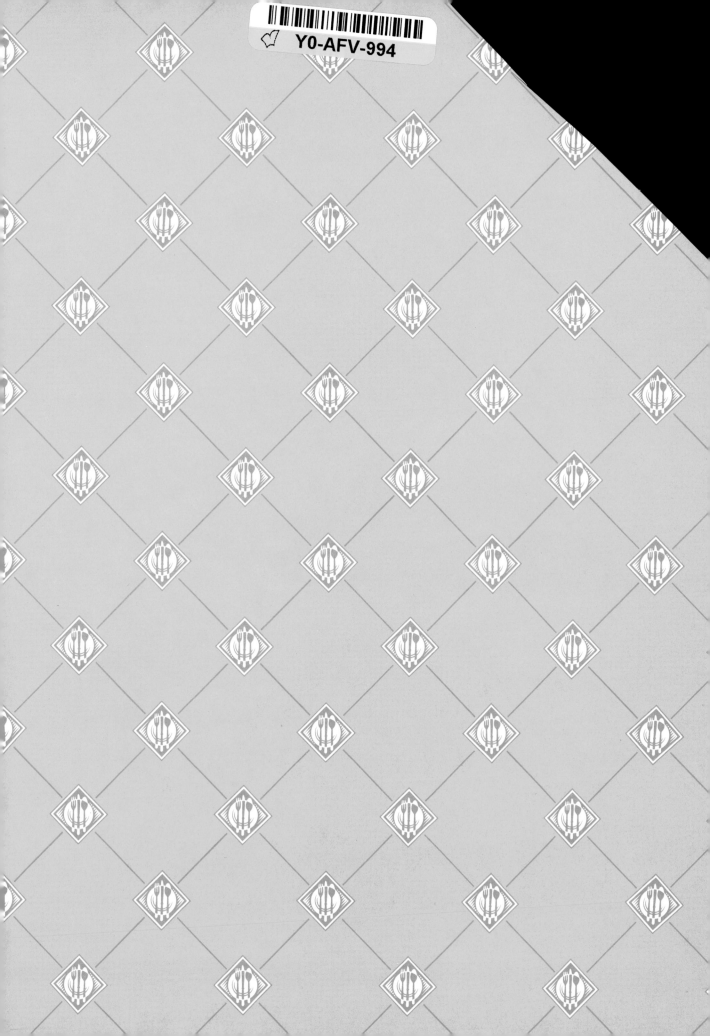

Hurry-Up

APPETIZER

RECIPES

Publications International, Ltd.

ISBN: 1-56173-973-1

Front cover photography by Sacco Productions Limited, Chicago.

Pictured on the front cover (*clockwise from top left*): Bacon Appetizer Crescents (*page 50*), Turkey Nachos Olé (*page 64*) and Vegetable Pita Pizzas (*page 54*).

Pictured on the back cover (*clockwise from top*): Broiled Shrimp Chutney (*page 25*), Seafood Ravioli with Fresh Tomato Sauce (*page 20*) and Sparkling White Sangria (page 40).

8 7 6 5 4 3 2 1

Manufactured in U.S.A.

Microwave ovens vary in wattage. The cooking times given in this publication are approximate. Use the cooking times as guidelines and check for doneness before adding more time. Consult manufacturer's instructions for suitable microwave-safe cooking dishes.

This edition published by Publications International, Ltd. 7373 N. Cicero Ave. Lincolnwood, IL 60646.

Hurry-Up APPETIZER RECIPES

Asparagus Cream Soup

- 2 tablespoons CRISCO® Shortening
- 1/4 cup chopped onion
- 2 packages (10 ounces each) frozen cut asparagus
- 1 cup chicken broth
- 4 egg yolks,* slightly beaten
- 2 1/2 cups milk
- 1 teaspoon salt
- 1/4 teaspoon pepper
- 4 drops hot pepper sauce

1. In medium saucepan melt Crisco®; add onion and cook until tender.

2. Add frozen asparagus and chicken broth; cook uncovered 10 minutes over high heat.

3. Transfer mixture to blender and purée. (Or force mixture through a fine wire sieve.) Add beaten egg yolks.

4. Return mixture to saucepan. Stir in milk, salt, pepper and hot pepper sauce. Reheat before serving; *do not boil*. ***Makes 1 1/2 quarts***

*Use clean, uncracked eggs.

Chilled Zucchini-Basil Soup

- 2 cups chicken broth
- 3 medium zucchini, sliced
- 2 medium onions, chopped
- 1 tablespoon minced fresh basil *or* 1 teaspoon dried basil
- 1 clove garlic, sliced
- 1/2 cup HELLMANN'S® or BEST FOODS® Real, Light or Cholesterol Free Reduced Calorie Mayonnaise
- 2 tablespoons lemon juice
- 1/8 teaspoon hot pepper sauce

In 3-quart saucepan combine chicken broth, zucchini, onions, basil and garlic. Bring to boil over high heat. Reduce heat to low; cover and simmer 10 minutes or until zucchini is tender. Cool. In blender or food processor container place zucchini mixture, half at a time. Process until smooth. Pour into large bowl. Stir in mayonnaise, lemon juice and hot pepper sauce until well blended. Cover; chill several hours or overnight.
Makes about 4 cups

Swiss Broccoli Soup

- 2 tablespoons minced onion
- 1 tablespoon butter or margarine
- 1 jar (12 ounces) HEINZ® HomeStyle Chicken Gravy
- 1 1/4 cups milk
- 1 package (10 ounces) frozen chopped broccoli, cooked, drained
- 1 cup shredded Swiss cheese Dash salt and pepper

In 2-quart saucepan, sauté onion in butter until tender. Stir in gravy, milk and broccoli; heat slowly, stirring occasionally. Add cheese, salt and pepper; heat until cheese is melted, stirring frequently.
Makes 4 servings (about 4 cups)

Swiss Broccoli Soup

Carrot-Rice Soup

Chilly Cucumber Soup

- 2 tablespoons butter or margarine
- 2 tablespoons all-purpose flour
- 4 large cucumbers, peeled, seeded and finely chopped (about 3½ cups)
- ¼ cup finely chopped parsley
- ¼ cup finely chopped celery leaves
- 1 envelope LIPTON® Recipe Secrets Golden Onion Recipe Soup Mix
- 2 cups water
- 2 cups (1 pint) light cream or half-and-half

In large saucepan, melt butter and cook flour over medium heat, stirring constantly, 3 minutes. Add cucumbers, parsley and celery leaves. Reduce heat to low and cook 8 minutes or until vegetables are tender. Stir in golden onion recipe soup mix thoroughly blended with water. Bring to a boil, then simmer covered 15 minutes. Remove from heat, then cool.

In food processor or blender, purée soup mixture. Stir in cream; chill. Serve cold and garnish, if desired, with cucumber slices and lemon peel.

Makes about 6 (1-cup) servings

Carrot-Rice Soup

- 1 pound carrots, peeled and chopped
- 1 medium onion, chopped
- 1 tablespoon margarine
- 4 cups chicken broth, divided
- ¼ teaspoon dried tarragon leaves
- ¼ teaspoon ground white pepper
- 2¼ cups cooked rice
- ¼ cup light sour cream
  Snipped parsley or mint for garnish

Cook carrots and onion in margarine in large saucepan or Dutch oven over medium-high heat 2 to 3 minutes or until onion is tender. Add 2 cups broth, tarragon, and pepper. Reduce heat; simmer 10 minutes. Combine vegetables and broth in food processor or blender; process until smooth. Return to saucepan. Add remaining 2 cups broth and rice; thoroughly heat. Dollop sour cream on each serving of soup. Garnish with parsley.

Makes 6 servings

Favorite recipe from **USA Rice Council**

Potato Soup

- 1 pound red potatoes (about 8 small), peeled, cut into ½-inch cubes
- 2 cups water
- ½ teaspoon salt
- ¼ cup BUTTER FLAVOR CRISCO®
- ¾ cup chopped celery
- ½ cup chopped onion
- 2 medium carrots, finely chopped
- 3 tablespoons all-purpose flour
- 3 cups milk
- ¾ teaspoon salt
- ¼ teaspoon white pepper
- ⅛ teaspoon dried thyme leaves

In 2-quart saucepan place potatoes, water and salt. Heat to boiling. Reduce heat; cover and simmer 10 to 15 minutes or until tender. Drain.

In large skillet melt Butter Flavor Crisco®. Add celery, onion and carrots. Cook and stir over medium heat until tender. Stir in flour. Add to potatoes in saucepan. Stir in milk, salt, white pepper and thyme. Cook and stir over medium heat until bubbly. Continue to cook and stir 1 minute or until thickened. Remove from heat.

Makes 4 to 6 servings

Wild Rice Soup

2 cups water
½ cup uncooked wild rice
½ teaspoon salt
3 tablespoons BUTTER FLAVOR CRISCO®
½ cup chopped green bell pepper
½ cup chopped celery
⅓ cup chopped onion
1 clove garlic, minced
2 tablespoons all-purpose flour
1½ teaspoons instant chicken bouillon granules
½ teaspoon salt
⅛ teaspoon pepper
⅛ teaspoon bouquet garni seasoning
¾ cup cubed fully cooked ham
1 medium carrot, grated
2 tablespoons snipped fresh parsley
2 cups milk
2 cups half-and-half

In 2-quart saucepan combine water, wild rice and salt. Heat to boiling. Reduce heat; cover and simmer 30 minutes or until tender. Drain in colander. Set aside. In 2-quart saucepan melt Butter Flavor Crisco®. Add green pepper, celery, onion and garlic. Cook and stir over medium heat about 7 minutes or until tender. Stir in flour, bouillon granules, salt, pepper and bouquet garni. Add cooked rice, ham, carrot, parsley, milk and half-and-half. Cook over medium heat 15 to 20 minutes or until very hot, stirring occasionally.

Makes 4 to 6 servings

Albondigas Soup

1 pound ground beef
¼ cup long-grain rice
1 egg
1 tablespoon chopped fresh cilantro
1 teaspoon LAWRY'S® Seasoned Salt
¼ cup ice water
2 cans (14½ ounces each) chicken broth
1 can (14½ ounces) whole peeled tomatoes, undrained and cut up
¼ cup chopped onion
1 stalk celery, diced
1 large carrot, diced
1 medium potato, diced
¼ teaspoon LAWRY'S® Garlic Powder with Parsley

In medium bowl, combine ground beef, rice, egg, cilantro, Seasoned Salt and ice water; form into small meatballs. In large saucepan, combine broth with vegetables and Garlic Powder with Parsley. Bring to a boil; add meatballs. Reduce heat, cover and simmer 30 to 40 minutes, stirring occasionally.

Makes 6 to 8 servings

Presentation: Serve with lemon wedges and warm tortillas.

Hint: For a lower salt version, use homemade chicken broth or low-sodium chicken broth.

Albondigas Soup

Dogwood Blossom Soup

- ½ cup (1 stick) unsalted butter
- 4 cups minced cauliflower (about 1 pound)
- 2 cups chopped onions
- 1 tablespoon CHEF PAUL PRUDHOMME'S VEGETABLE MAGIC®
- 4 cups chicken broth or water, in all
- 6 ounces cooked ham, minced
- 2 bay leaves
- ¼ teaspoon ground nutmeg
- 4 cups heavy cream, in all
- 6 cups very small cauliflowerets (no larger than ½ inch)

Dogwood Blossom Soup

In 5-quart saucepan over medium-high heat, melt butter. When butter comes to a hard sizzle, stir in minced cauliflower and onions. Reduce heat to medium. Cook about 14 minutes, stirring occasionally. Let mixture stick slightly but not brown. Stir in Vegetable Magic® and cook 13 minutes more, stirring occasionally and more frequently toward end of cooking time, again taking care not to let mixture brown. Stir in 2 cups of the broth and cook about 10 minutes, stirring occasionally. Add ham, bay leaves and nutmeg. Stir well and cook about 5 minutes.

Add the remaining 2 cups broth, stir well and cook 7 minutes more or until mixture comes to a rolling boil. Whisk in 2 cups of the cream and cook, whisking occasionally, about 8 minutes or until cream has reduced and thickened somewhat.

Whisk in the remaining 2 cups cream and cook, whisking frequently, about 12 minutes or until soup has reduced and thickened enough to coat a spoon. Add cauliflowerets and cook, whisking frequently, 10 minutes or until soup comes to a boil. Reduce heat to low and cook, whisking occasionally, 10 minutes or until cauliflowerets are tender yet still firm.

Let soup set 10 to 15 minutes before serving for flavors to blend. Remove bay leaves before serving.

Makes about 10 cups

Salsa Corn Chowder

- Cook and stir onions in margarine in large saucepan. Stir in flour and seasonings.
- Add corn, salsa, broth and pimento. Bring to boil; remove from heat.
- Gradually add ¼ cup hot mixture to cream cheese in small bowl, stirring until well blended.
- Add cream cheese mixture and milk to saucepan, stirring until well blended.
- Cook until thoroughly heated. *Do not boil.* Top each serving with sprig of cilantro. Serve immediately.

Makes 6 to 8 servings

Microwave: • Microwave onions and margarine in 3-quart casserole on HIGH 2 to 3 minutes or until onions are tender. • Stir in flour and seasonings. • Add salsa and broth; mix well. • Microwave 8 to 10 minutes or until mixture begins to boil, stirring after 5 minutes. • Stir in corn and pimento. • Add ¼ cup hot mixture to cream cheese in small bowl, stirring until well blended.
• Add cream cheese mixture and milk to corn mixture. • Microwave 12 to 17 minutes or until thoroughly heated, stirring after 9 minutes. Do not boil. Top each serving with sprig of cilantro. Serve immediately.

Salsa Corn Chowder

Preparation Time: 35 minutes

1½ cups chopped onions
2 tablespoons PARKAY® Margarine
1 tablespoon flour
1 tablespoon chili powder
1 teaspoon ground cumin
1 package (16 ounces) BIRDS EYE® Sweet Corn, thawed
2 cups salsa
1 can (13¾ ounces) chicken broth
1 jar (4 ounces) chopped pimento, drained
1 container (8 ounces) PHILADELPHIA BRAND® Soft Cream Cheese
1 cup milk
Cilantro

Left: Chilled Avocado Soup; Right: Corn & Red Pepper Soup

Chilled Avocado Soup

  3 **small onion slices, each**
     ¼ **inch thick, divided**
  1 **can (14½ ounces) ready-to-**
     serve chicken broth
½ **cup plain yogurt**
1½ **tablespoons lemon juice**
  1 **large ripe avocado, halved**
     and pitted
  3 **to 5 drops hot pepper sauce**
     Salt
     White pepper
¼ **cup finely chopped tomato**
¼ **cup finely chopped cucumber**
     Cilantro sprigs for garnish

Place 1 onion slice, chicken broth, yogurt and lemon juice in blender or food processor; process until well blended. Remove flesh from avocado; spoon into blender. Process until smooth. Pour into medium container with tight-fitting lid. Add hot pepper sauce and salt and pepper to taste. Finely chop the remaining 2 onion slices; add to soup. Stir in tomato and cucumber. Cover and refrigerate 2 hours or up to 24 hours. Serve in individual bowls. Garnish with cilantro and additional chopped tomato and cucumber if desired.

Makes 6 servings

Corn & Red Pepper Soup

2 tablespoons butter or
    margarine
2 cups seeded and coarsely
    chopped red bell peppers
1 medium onion, thinly sliced
1 can (14½ ounces) ready-to-
    serve chicken broth
1 package (10 ounces) frozen
    whole kernel corn (see Note)
½ teaspoon ground cumin
½ cup sour cream
    Salt
    White pepper
    Sunflower seeds for garnish

Melt butter in 3-quart saucepan over medium heat. Add bell peppers and onion; cook until tender. Add chicken broth, corn and cumin. Bring to a boil. Cover; reduce heat and simmer 20 minutes or until corn is tender. Pour into blender or food processor; process until smooth. Place sieve over bowl; pour corn mixture into sieve. Press mixture with rubber spatula to extract all liquid. Discard pulp. Return liquid to pan; whisk in sour cream until evenly blended. Add salt and pepper to taste. Reheat but do not boil. Serve in individual bowls. Garnish with sunflower seeds.

Makes 4 servings

Note: If you wish to make this with fresh corn, cut the raw kernels from four large ears of yellow or white corn.

Scandinavian Raspberry Soup

2 (10-ounce) packages frozen
    red raspberries in syrup,
    thawed
½ cup orange juice
¼ cup REALEMON® Lemon Juice
    from Concentrate
1 tablespoon cornstarch
1 tablespoon sugar, optional
¾ cup chablis or other dry white
    wine
    Fresh orange sections
    Raspberries, orange peel twists
    or mint leaves, optional
    BORDEN® or MEADOW GOLD®
    Sour Cream

In blender or food processor, purée *1 package* raspberries; strain to remove seeds. In medium saucepan, combine puréed raspberries, orange juice, ReaLemon® brand, cornstarch and sugar if desired; mix well. Over medium heat, cook and stir until slightly thickened and clear; cool. Stir in remaining *1 package* raspberries and wine. Cover; chill. To serve, place several orange sections in each bowl; add soup. Garnish with raspberries, orange twists or mint leaves; serve with sour cream. Refrigerate leftovers.

Makes about 3 cups

French Onion Soup

1 extra large onion (1 pound)
3 tablespoons BUTTER FLAVOR
    CRISCO®
1 clove garlic, minced
1 tablespoon all-purpose flour
5 cups water
¼ cup white wine, optional
3 tablespoons instant beef
    bouillon granules
1 tablespoon instant chicken
    bouillon granules
1 teaspoon Worcestershire sauce
    Seasoned croutons
    Grated Parmesan cheese

Peel onion. Cut in half lengthwise, then crosswise into thin slices.

In 3-quart saucepan melt Butter Flavor Crisco®. Add onion and garlic. Cook over medium heat about 20 minutes or until onion is soft and transparent, stirring occasionally. Stir in flour. Add water, wine, beef and chicken bouillon granules and Worcestershire sauce. Heat to boiling. Reduce heat; cover and simmer 15 minutes.

Ladle soup into individual serving bowls. Top with seasoned croutons and sprinkle with Parmesan cheese.

Makes 4 to 6 servings

Shrimp Louie

- ½ head iceberg lettuce, shredded
- 8 ounces tiny cooked shrimp
- 1 can (8¼ ounces) DEL MONTE® Sliced Beets, drained
- 1 can (15 ounces) DEL MONTE® All Green Asparagus Spears, drained
- 2 hard-cooked eggs, sliced
- 8 pitted ripe olives
  Louie Dressing (recipe follows)

Place lettuce on serving platter. Arrange shrimp, beets, asparagus and eggs over lettuce. Garnish with olives. Serve with Louie Dressing. Garnish with sliced green onions or chopped parsley, if desired.

Makes 4 servings

Louie Dressing

- ½ cup mayonnaise
- ⅓ cup DEL MONTE® Seafood Cocktail Sauce
- 1 tablespoon lemon juice
- ¼ cup chopped green pepper
- 2 tablespoons chopped green onion

Blend together mayonnaise, cocktail sauce and lemon juice. Stir in pepper and onion. Chill. Serve with Shrimp Louie. Remaining dressing may be refrigerated and served with other salads.

Makes about 1 cup

Black Bean Spirals

Preparation Time: 15 minutes plus refrigerating

- 4 ounces PHILADELPHIA BRAND® Cream Cheese, softened
- ½ cup (2 ounces) 100% Natural KRAFT® Shredded Monterey Jack Cheese with Jalapeño Peppers
- ¼ cup sour cream
- ¼ teaspoon onion salt
- 1 cup canned black beans, rinsed, drained
- 3 flour tortillas (10-inch)
  Salsa

- Beat cheeses, sour cream and onion salt in small mixing bowl at medium speed with electric mixer until well blended.

- Place beans in food processor container fitted with steel blade or blender; process until smooth. Spread thin layer of beans onto each tortilla; spread cheese mixture over beans.

- Roll tortillas up tightly; refrigerate 30 minutes. Cut into ½-inch slices. Serve with salsa.

Makes 12 servings

Harvest Vegetable Platter with Orange-Walnut Sauce

1 small acorn squash, halved, seeded and cut into ¼-inch-thick slices
2 cups broccoli florets and sliced stems
2 cups cauliflower florets
2 cups ¼-inch-thick carrot slices (4 to 6 medium)
Orange-Walnut Sauce (recipe follows)

Arrange acorn squash slices in overlapping pattern around the outside edge of a large microwave-safe platter. Arrange a row of broccoli next to the squash, then a row of cauliflower. Place sliced carrots in the center. Cover with plastic wrap, venting one corner. Microwave on HIGH 8 to 10 minutes, turning twice, until vegetables are tender, but still crisp. Let stand 5 minutes. Pour off any liquid from platter. Pour Orange-Walnut Sauce over vegetables and serve.

Makes 6 to 8 servings

Harvest Vegetable Platter with Orange-Walnut Sauce

Orange-Walnut Sauce

½ cup butter or margarine
¼ cup orange juice concentrate
¼ cup minced green onion
2 tablespoons Dijon mustard
¼ teaspoon red pepper flakes (optional)
¾ cup chopped walnuts

Place butter, orange juice concentrate, green onion, mustard and red pepper flakes in 4-cup glass measure. Microwave on HIGH 2 minutes or until butter is melted. Add walnuts and stir until combined.

Note: Sauce may be made up to 3 days ahead and refrigerated in sealed container. To reheat, microwave on HIGH 2 minutes and stir before serving.

Favorite recipe from **The Walnut Marketing Board**

Garlic and Shrimp Appetizer

½ cup butter or margarine, softened
2 tablespoons finely chopped parsley
4 teaspoons finely chopped shallots
4 cloves finely chopped fresh garlic
2 teaspoons Pernod®
½ teaspoon lemon juice
¼ teaspoon paprika
⅛ teaspoon cayenne pepper
⅛ teaspoon salt
1½ pounds shrimp, shelled and deveined
Flour
⅓ cup olive or vegetable oil
½ of fresh lemon
¾ cup dry white wine

Cream butter using a wooden spoon. Add parsley, shallots, garlic, Pernod®, lemon juice, paprika, cayenne pepper and salt; blend well. Coat shrimp with flour. Heat the olive oil in a large skillet. Shake the flour from the shrimp and add shrimp to the skillet. Cook for about 3 minutes. When they start to turn pink, turn them and cook on the other side. Drain the oil from the skillet; squeeze the lemon over shrimp, add the wine and stir over high heat for about 1 minute. Add the butter mixture and toss quickly using a wooden spoon. When the butter is melted, serve the shrimp immediately sprinkled with additional chopped parsley if desired. **Makes 4 to 6 servings**

Favorite recipe from **Fresh Garlic Association**

Tex-Mex Cheese Fondue with Turkey

 ½ **pound low-fat Swiss cheese, grated**
 ½ **pound low-fat Monterey Jack cheese, grated**
 2 **tablespoons flour**
 1 **clove garlic, peeled and halved**
 1¼ **cups Mexican beer**
 ¼ **cup fresh cilantro, chopped**
 1 **jalapeño pepper, chopped**
 ½ **pound turkey ham, cut into ³⁄₄-inch cubes**
 ½ **pound turkey kielbasa or smoked turkey sausage, cut into ½-inch slices**
   Unsalted tortilla chips
   Assorted cut-up vegetables such as jícama and chayote

1. In medium-size bowl, combine Swiss cheese, Monterey Jack cheese and flour.

2. In bottom and sides of fondue pot or 2-quart saucepan rub garlic; discard remaining garlic. Add beer, cilantro and jalapeño pepper. Over medium-high heat, cook mixture until it begins to bubble. Reduce heat to medium and gradually add cheese mixture, stirring until smooth and creamy.

3. Place fondue pot over flame and serve with turkey ham, turkey kielbasa, tortilla chips and assorted vegetables as dippers.
Makes about 3 cups sauce or 8 to 10 servings

Favorite recipe from **National Turkey Federation**

Shrimp Antipasto

Shrimp Antipasto

 1½ **pounds medium raw shrimp, peeled, deveined and cooked**
 6 **ounces Provolone cheese, cut into cubes**
 1 **(6-ounce) can pitted ripe olives, drained**
 1 **cup vegetable oil**
 ⅔ **cup REALEMON® Lemon Juice from Concentrate**
 2 **tablespoons Dijon-style mustard**
 2 **teaspoons sugar**
 1½ **teaspoons thyme leaves**
 1 **teaspoon salt**
 4 **ounces Genoa salami, cut into cubes**
 1 **large red bell pepper, cut into 1-inch pieces**

Place shrimp, cheese and olives in large shallow dish. Combine remaining ingredients except salami and bell pepper; mix well. Pour over shrimp mixture. Cover; marinate in refrigerator 6 hours or overnight, stirring occasionally. Add salami and bell pepper; toss. Drain; garnish as desired. Refrigerate leftovers.
Makes about 8 cups

Tip: Cooked scallops can be substituted for all or part of the shrimp.

Seviche

1 pound sole *or* haddock fillets, fresh or frozen, thawed, cut into bite-size pieces
2/3 cup REALIME® Lime Juice from Concentrate
1/4 cup sliced green onions
1 (2-ounce) jar sliced pimientos, drained and chopped
2 tablespoons water
1 clove garlic, finely chopped
1 teaspoon salt
1/4 teaspoon black pepper
    Dash hot pepper sauce
2 cups shredded lettuce

In plastic bag or medium bowl, combine all ingredients except lettuce. Cover; marinate in refrigerator 6 hours or overnight. Drain; serve on lettuce. Refrigerate leftovers.   ***Makes about 2 cups***

Prosciutto Fruit Bundles in Endive

2 tablespoons rice or white wine vinegar
1 tablespoon vegetable oil
1 tablespoon light soy sauce
1 green onion, sliced
1 (4-inch) rib celery, sliced
1/2 teaspoon sugar
1/2 teaspoon grated lime peel
1/4 teaspoon ground ginger
4 slices (3 x 1/2 inch) *each*: cantaloupe, pineapple, honeydew melon
8 julienne strips (2 x 1/4 inch) *each*: celery, green and red bell pepper
3 ounces thinly sliced domestic prosciutto ham
24 Belgian endive leaves

For dressing, combine vinegar, oil, soy sauce, green onion, celery, sugar, lime peel and ginger in blender or food processor; cover and blend until fairly smooth. Place fruits and vegetables in plastic bag. Add dressing; turn to coat. Close bag securely and marinate in refrigerator 30 minutes. Meanwhile, trim excess fat from ham and discard; cut ham lengthwise into 1/2-inch-wide strips. Remove fruits and vegetables from dressing. Wrap ham strips around following combinations: cantaloupe/2 strips celery; pineapple/2 strips green pepper; honeydew melon/2 strips red pepper. Place each bundle on endive leaf. Cover with plastic wrap and refrigerate until serving.
     Makes 24 appetizers

Favorite recipe from **National Live Stock & Meat Board**

Fettuccine Alfredo with Shiitake Mushrooms

1 tablespoon olive or vegetable oil
2 medium cloves garlic, finely chopped
1 cup sliced shiitake or white mushrooms
2 tablespoons dry white wine
1 tablespoon finely chopped fresh basil leaves*
1 1/2 cups milk
1 cup canned crushed tomatoes
1/2 cup water
1 package LIPTON® Noodles & Sauce—Alfredo
    Dash pepper

In 1 1/2-quart microwave-safe casserole, microwave olive oil with garlic, uncovered, at HIGH (Full Power) 1 minute. Add mushrooms, wine and basil and microwave 1 1/2 minutes or until mushrooms are tender. Stir in remaining ingredients and microwave at HIGH 13 to 14 minutes or until noodles are tender. Let stand 5 minutes. Garnish, if desired, with additional basil leaves and cherry tomatoes.
     Makes about 4 servings

*Substitution: Use 1/2 teaspoon dried basil leaves.

Conventional Directions: In medium skillet, heat oil and cook garlic over medium heat 30 seconds. Add mushrooms, wine and basil and cook over medium heat, stirring occasionally, 2 minutes or until mushrooms are tender. Stir in remaining ingredients plus 2 tablespoons Imperial® Margarine. Bring to a boil, then continue boiling, stirring occasionally, 8 minutes or until noodles are tender.

Jumbo Shells Seafood Fancies

Jumbo Shells Seafood Fancies

- 1 (16-ounce) package uncooked jumbo-sized pasta shells
- 1 (7½-ounce) can crabmeat, drained, flaked and cartilage removed
- 1 (2½-ounce) can tiny shrimp, drained
- 1 cup (4 ounces) shredded Swiss cheese
- ½ cup salad dressing or mayonnaise
- 2 tablespoons thinly sliced celery
- 1 tablespoon finely chopped onion
- 1 tablespoon finely chopped pimiento
- Celery leaves, for garnish

Add the shells gradually to 6 quarts of boiling salted water and cook until tender, yet firm. Drain; rinse with cold water, then drain again. Set aside, upside down, to cool. Combine the crabmeat, shrimp, cheese, salad dressing, celery, onion and pimiento in a small bowl. If the mixture seems too dry, add more salad dressing. Spoon the mixture into the cooled shells; cover and refrigerate until chilled. Serve the shells garnished with celery leaves. **Makes 8 to 10 servings**

Favorite recipe from **North Dakota Wheat Commission**

Crab Grande

Preparation Time: 15 minutes

- ½ cup chopped onion
- 2 tablespoons PARKAY® Margarine
- 1 pound VELVEETA® Mexican Pasteurized Process Cheese Spread with Jalapeño Pepper, cubed
- 1 can (8 ounces) tomatoes, cut up, drained
  Tortilla chips
- 2 cups shredded lettuce
- ⅓ cup pitted ripe olive slices
- 1 can (6 ounces) crabmeat, drained, flaked
  Sour cream
  Guacamole

- In saucepan, sauté onions in margarine.

- Add process cheese spread and tomatoes; stir until process cheese spread is melted.

- Place chips on serving platter; cover with lettuce, olives, process cheese spread mixture and crabmeat. Top with sour cream and guacamole.

Makes 6 to 8 servings

Variation: Substitute tuna for crabmeat.

Scallops Primavera

- 1 pound scallops
- ¼ cup REALEMON® Lemon Juice from Concentrate
- 1 cup thinly sliced carrots
- 3 cloves garlic, finely chopped
- ⅓ cup margarine or butter
- 8 ounces fresh mushrooms, sliced (about 2 cups)
- ¾ teaspoon thyme leaves
- 2 teaspoons cornstarch
- ½ teaspoon salt
- ¼ cup diagonally sliced green onions
- 4 ounces fresh pea pods *or* (6-ounce) package frozen pea pods, thawed
- 2 tablespoons dry sherry

Scallops Primavera

In shallow baking dish, marinate scallops in ReaLemon® brand 30 minutes, stirring occasionally. In large skillet, over high heat, cook and stir carrots and garlic in margarine until tender-crisp, about 3 minutes. Add mushrooms and thyme; cook and stir about 5 minutes. Stir cornstarch and salt into scallop mixture; add to skillet. Cook and stir until scallops are opaque, about 4 minutes. Add green onions, pea pods and sherry; heat through. Refrigerate leftovers.

Makes 4 servings

Mexican Sausage Pie

Preparation Time: 20 minutes
Cooking Time: 40 minutes plus
standing time

½ **pound chorizo sausage**
1 **pound loaf frozen whole**
   wheat bread dough, thawed
1 **package (10 ounces) BIRDS**
   EYE® Chopped Broccoli,
   thawed, well drained
1 **cup BIRDS EYE® Sweet Corn,**
   thawed, well drained
½ **pound VELVEETA® Mexican**
   Pasteurized Process Cheese
   Spread with Jalapeño
   Pepper, sliced
1 **egg yolk**
1 **teaspoon cold water**
1 **tablespoon cornmeal**

- Heat oven to 375°.
- Remove sausage from casing. Brown sausage; drain. Cool.
- Roll two thirds of dough to 11-inch circle on lightly floured surface. Press onto bottom and up sides of greased 9-inch springform pan.
- Layer broccoli, corn, sausage and process cheese spread over dough in pan.
- Roll remaining dough to 10-inch circle; cut into 8 wedges. Place over filling, overlapping edges and sealing ends to bottom crust. Brush with combined egg yolk and water. Sprinkle with cornmeal.
- Bake 35 to 40 minutes or until deep golden brown. Let stand 10 minutes. **Makes 10 servings**

Mexican Sausage Pie

Seafood Ravioli with Fresh Tomato Sauce

Seafood Ravioli with Fresh Tomato Sauce

Preparation Time: 25 minutes
Cooking Time: 3 minutes per batch

  1 container (8 ounces)
     PHILADELPHIA BRAND® Soft
     Cream Cheese with Herb &
     Garlic
3/4 cup chopped LOUIS KEMP®
     CRAB DELIGHTS Chunks,
     rinsed
36 wonton wrappers
     Cold water
     Fresh Tomato Sauce

- Stir cream cheese and crab flavored surimi seafood in medium bowl until well blended.

- For each ravioli, place 1 tablespoonful cream cheese mixture in center of one wonton wrapper. Brush edges with water. Place second wonton wrapper on top. Press edges together to seal, taking care to press out air. Repeat with remaining cream cheese mixture and wonton wrappers.

- For square-shaped ravioli, cut edges of wonton wrappers with pastry trimmer to form square. For round-shaped ravioli, place 3-inch round biscuit cutter on ravioli, making sure center of each cutter contains filling. Press down firmly, cutting through both wrappers, to trim edges. Repeat with remaining ravioli.

- Bring 1½ quarts water to boil in large saucepan. Cook ravioli, a few at a time, 2 to 3 minutes or until they rise to surface. Remove with slotted spoon. Serve hot with Fresh Tomato Sauce. ***Makes 18***

Fresh Tomato Sauce

  2 garlic cloves, minced
  2 tablespoons olive oil
  6 plum tomatoes, diced
  1 tablespoon red wine vinegar
  1 tablespoon chopped parsley

- Cook and stir garlic in oil in medium saucepan 1 minute. Add remaining ingredients.

- Cook over low heat 2 to 3 minutes or until thoroughly heated, stirring occasionally. Cool to room temperature.

Variation: For triangle-shaped ravioli, place 2 teaspoonfuls cream cheese mixture in center of each wonton wrapper; brush edges with water. Fold in half to form triangle. Press edges together to seal, taking care to press out air. Trim edges of wonton wrapper with pastry trimmer, if desired. ***Makes 36***

Scallops in Hot Sauce

  1/4 cup olive or vegetable oil
  5 cloves garlic, coarsely
     chopped
  1 pound bay scallops
3/4 cup slivered red bell peppers
3/4 cup slivered green bell
     peppers
1/2 cup chopped onion
1/2 teaspoon TABASCO® Brand
     Pepper Sauce
1/4 teaspoon salt
  2 tablespoons drained capers

In large skillet heat oil; sauté garlic until golden. Add scallops, peppers, onion, Tabasco® Sauce and salt. Cook, stirring constantly, until scallops turn opaque and vegetables are crisp-tender. Stir in capers. Serve hot.

Makes about 4 cups

Seafood Cocktails with Watercress Sauce

- 1 large bunch watercress, stems removed (about 2 cups loosely packed)*
- 1 small bunch parsley, stems removed (about 1 cup loosely packed)*
- 1 medium clove garlic, finely chopped
- 1 envelope LIPTON® Recipe Secrets Golden Onion Recipe Soup Mix
- 1/2 pint (8 ounces) sour cream
- 1/4 cup mayonnaise
- 1/8 teaspoon pepper
  Suggested Seafood**

In food processor or blender, combine watercress, parsley and garlic until blended. Add golden onion recipe soup mix, sour cream, mayonnaise and pepper; process until smooth. Chill at least 2 hours. Serve with Suggested Seafood. Garnish as desired.

Makes about 2 cups sauce or about 8 appetizer servings

*Variation: Omit watercress. Use 2 small bunches parsley, stems removed (about 2 cups loosely packed).

**Suggested Seafood: Use about 2 pounds cooked and chilled butterflied shrimp, scallops, crab claws and legs, lobster meat or clams.

Crab Salad Cocktail

- 1 pound cooked crabmeat, flaked
- 3 tablespoons minced fresh parsley
- 1/4 cup FILIPPO BERIO® Extra Virgin Olive Oil
  Juice from 1 large lemon
- 1/4 teaspoon white pepper
  Crab shells or cherry tomatoes

1. Shred the crabmeat in a bowl with a fork and combine with parsley.

2. Add oil and lemon juice. Sprinkle with white pepper. Stuff crab shells or hollowed out cherry tomatoes with crab mixture. Chill thoroughly before serving.   **Makes 4 servings**

Preparation Time: 10 minutes

Walnut Tomatoes Romany

- 4 tomatoes (about 3 inches in diameter)
- 3 tablespoons red wine vinegar
- 2 tablespoons olive or vegetable oil
- 2 tablespoons chopped fresh basil or 1½ teaspoons dried basil
- 1 clove garlic, minced
- 1/4 teaspoon salt
- 1/8 teaspoon pepper
- 4 ounces mozzarella cheese, cut into 1/2-inch cubes
- 1/2 cup coarsely chopped walnuts
  Walnut halves and pieces, for garnish

With small knife, remove stem ends from tomatoes. Halve tomatoes vertically. Remove pulp with melon baller or knife. Cut pulp into 1/2-inch pieces. Cover and reserve tomato shells. In medium bowl whisk vinegar and oil. Mix in basil, garlic, salt and pepper. Add tomato pieces and cheese; toss. Cover and chill 1 to 2 hours. Mix chopped walnuts into tomato-cheese mixture, then fill tomato shells. Garnish with walnut halves and pieces.

Makes 4 servings

Favorite recipe from **The Walnut Marketing Board**

Seafood Cocktails with Watercress Sauce

PARTY PERFECT

Southwestern Cheesecake

*Preparation Time: 20 minutes
plus refrigerating
Cooking Time: 30 minutes*

1 cup finely crushed tortilla chips
3 tablespoons PARKAY®
   Margarine, melted
2 packages (8 ounces each)
   PHILADELPHIA BRAND® Cream
   Cheese, softened
2 eggs
1 package (8 ounces) 100%
   Natural KRAFT® Shredded
   Colby/Monterey Jack
   Cheese
1 can (4 ounces) chopped
   green chilies, drained
1 cup sour cream
1 cup chopped yellow or
   orange bell pepper
½ cup sliced green onion
⅓ cup chopped tomatoes
¼ cup pitted ripe olive slices

- Heat oven to 325°F.

- Stir chips and margarine in small bowl; press onto bottom of 9-inch springform pan. Bake 15 minutes.

- Beat cream cheese and eggs in large mixing bowl at medium speed with electric mixer until well blended. Mix in shredded cheese and chilies; pour over crust. Bake 30 minutes.

- Spread sour cream over cheesecake. Loosen cake from rim of pan; cool before removing rim of pan. Refrigerate.

- Top with remaining ingredients just before serving.
   Makes 16 to 20 servings

Honey-Dijon Brie

3 tablespoons GREY POUPON®
   Dijon Mustard
2 tablespoons honey
2 tablespoons chopped parsley
1 sheet unbaked frozen puff
   pastry, thawed
1 (1-pound) round Brie, halved
   horizontally
1 egg, beaten with 1 teaspoon
   water
   Green curly leaf lettuce, for
   garnish

In bowl, blend mustard, honey and parsley; set aside.

Roll out puff pastry to 12-inch square; cut a 1-inch strip from one edge and reserve for decoration. Spoon half the mustard mixture in 6-inch circle on center of pastry. Place one half of the Brie, top-side down, on mustard mixture; spread with remaining mustard sauce. Top with remaining Brie, cut-side down. Bring edges of pastry together over cheese, sealing well.

Place seam-side down on ungreased baking sheet. Brush with egg mixture. Cut desired shapes from reserved pastry; arrange on top. Brush again with egg mixture. Bake at 400°F for 20 to 25 minutes or until golden. Let stand at least 30 minutes before serving. Serve on lettuce-lined platter. (May be prepared early in the day and warmed slightly before serving.)
Makes 8 servings

Easy Mexican Cheese Twirls

*Preparation Time: 15 minutes
plus refrigerating*

1/2 pound VELVEETA® Mexican Pasteurized Process Cheese Spread with Jalapeño Pepper
1 package (8 ounces) PHILADELPHIA BRAND® Cream Cheese, softened
2 tablespoons chopped pitted ripe olives
1 tablespoon chopped cilantro

• Roll process cheese spread between 2 pieces of wax paper to form 12x9-inch rectangle.

• Beat cream cheese, olives and cilantro until well blended. Spread over process cheese spread.

• Roll up, starting at narrow end, to form 9-inch roll. Garnish with additional cilantro, if desired. Wrap in plastic wrap; chill until firm. Cut into 1/4-inch slices. Serve with assorted crackers.

Makes about 36 appetizers

Spicy Beef Pita Sandwiches

Spicy Beef Pita Sandwiches

1/2 pound cooked roast beef, sliced 1/8 inch thick
3/4 cup bottled Italian dressing
1/3 cup sliced green onion
1 tablespoon prepared mustard
2 medium red or green bell peppers, cut into strips
1/4 pound Swiss cheese slices, cut into 1/4-inch strips
1/3 cup mayonnaise
6 pita pocket breads, cut in half Leaf lettuce
2 medium tomatoes, sliced Alfalfa sprouts, if desired

Cut beef into 1/2-inch-wide strips. Combine dressing, green onion and mustard in medium-size bowl. Add roast beef and peppers; mix well. Cover; chill several hours or overnight, stirring occasionally. Immediately before serving, drain beef mixture, reserving dressing. Add cheese to drained beef mixture, tossing lightly. Combine mayonnaise with reserved dressing; mix well. Open pita bread halves; line with lettuce and tomato. Fill with beef and cheese mixture. Top each with mayonnaise mixture and sprouts, if desired. Serve immediately.

Makes 12 sandwich halves

Broiled Shrimp Chutney

Broiled Shrimp Chutney

- **1 pound medium shrimp, shelled and deveined**
- **1/2 cup HELLMANN'S® or BEST FOODS® Real, Light or Cholesterol Free Reduced Calorie Mayonnaise, divided**
- **1/2 teaspoon crushed dried red pepper**
- **1/4 cup minced red onion**
- **2 tablespoons chutney, finely chopped**
- **1/2 teaspoon grated lime peel**
- **2 tablespoons lime juice**
- **1 teaspoon grated fresh ginger**

In medium bowl toss shrimp with 1/4 cup of the mayonnaise and the dried red pepper. In shallow baking pan broil shrimp 5 inches from heat, turning once, 4 minutes or until pink. Cool slightly; chop finely. In medium bowl toss shrimp with remaining 1/4 cup mayonnaise, the onion, chutney, lime peel, lime juice and ginger. Cover; chill at least 1 hour. Serve on cucumber slices, rice crackers or wrapped in lettuce leaves. Garnish as desired.

Makes 1 1/2 cups

Sherried Turkey Cocktail Meatballs

Try

- **2 pounds TURKEY SAUSAGE**
- **2/3 cup seasoned bread crumbs**
- **1 bottle (9 ounces) mango chutney**
- **1 cup low-fat plain yogurt**
- **1/3 cup dry sherry**

1. Preheat oven to 375°F.

2. In medium bowl combine sausage and bread crumbs. Form mixture into 1-inch balls. Arrange meatballs on two (15×10 inch) baking pans. Bake 25 to 30 minutes or until meatballs are no longer pink in center.

3. In blender or food processor puree chutney until smooth. In small saucepan, over low heat, combine chutney, yogurt and sherry; cook until mixture is slightly thickened. *Do not boil.*

4. To serve, combine meatballs and sauce in chafing dish.

Makes about 80 meatballs

Favorite recipe from **National Turkey Federation**

Italian Salad Bundles

Italian Salad Bundles

*Preparation Time: 30 minutes
plus refrigerating*

  5 green onions
  1 cup cooked orzo or rice
  1/2 cup seeded diced tomato
  1/2 cup diced zucchini
  1/3 cup KRAFT® House Italian
    Dressing
  1/4 pound VELVEETA® Pasteurized
    Process Cheese Spread, cut
    into small cubes
  16 OSCAR MAYER® Cotto Salami
    Slices

• Cut green tops from onions;
  reserve for later use. Chop white
  bottoms.

• Mix together chopped onions,
  orzo, tomato, zucchini and
  dressing. Refrigerate 1 hour.

• Add process cheese spread; toss
  lightly.

• Blanch onion tops in boiling water
  30 seconds or until softened.

• For each bundle, place 2
  tablespoons orzo mixture in center
  of one salami slice; roll up. Tie with
  green onion top.

Makes 16 appetizers

Mini Smoked Turkey & Swiss Sandwiches

Preparation Time: 30 minutes

  1 1/2 cups MIRACLE WHIP® Salad
    Dressing
  3 tablespoons *each:* chopped
    green onions, KRAFT®
    Prepared Horseradish
  1 1/2 tablespoons Dijon mustard
  48 dinner rolls or miniature buns,
    split
    Lettuce
  2 (12-ounce) packages smoked
    turkey breast slices
  1 (16-ounce) package 100%
    Natural KRAFT® Swiss Cheese
    Slices, cut into thirds

• Mix together salad dressing,
  onions, horseradish and mustard
  until well blended.

• Spread rolls with salad dressing
  mixture; fill with lettuce, turkey and
  cheese.   **Makes 4 dozen**

Nutty Cheese-Beef Crudités

Preparation Time: 10 minutes
Microwave Cooking Time:
8½ to 10 minutes

¼ cup chopped walnuts
8 ounces ground beef
3 ounces Neufchatel cream
   cheese, softened
3 tablespoons finely chopped
   green onion with tops
¼ teaspoon salt
   Dash of pepper
24 vegetable pieces (zucchini,
   cucumber or jícama slices;
   red, green or yellow bell
   pepper, cut into 1½-inch
   squares; or pea pods,
   blanched and split)
1 tablespoon sliced green onion
   with top

Place walnuts in 1-cup microwave-safe glass measure. Microwave at HIGH 4 to 5 minutes or until lightly browned, stirring after 2 minutes; set aside. Break up ground beef with fork; place in microwave-safe sieve or colander. Place sieve in microwave-safe bowl. Microwave at HIGH 2½ minutes. Pour off drippings and place beef in same bowl. Stir in Neufchatel cheese, chopped green onion, walnuts, salt and pepper. Microwave at HIGH 2 to 2½ minutes. Top or fill desired vegetable pieces with 1 rounded teaspoon meat mixture. Garnish each appetizer with sliced green onion.

Makes 24 appetizers

Favorite recipe from **National Live Stock & Meat Board**

Country Style Paté in French Bread

Try

Preparation Time: 25 minutes

1 (12-inch) French bread loaf
1 (8-ounce) package
   braunschweiger liver
   sausage
½ cup MIRACLE WHIP® Salad
   Dressing
⅓ cup finely chopped pistachio
   nuts or walnuts
1 tablespoon *each:* chopped
   onion, chopped fresh
   parsley
½ teaspoon dry mustard

- Slice off both ends of bread loaf. Cut loaf into fourths. Remove bread from inside of each fourth leaving ½-inch shell. Tear removed bread into small pieces.

- Mix together torn bread with remaining ingredients until well blended.

- Lightly pack about ⅓ cup liver sausage mixture into each bread piece.

- Wrap securely in plastic wrap; chill several hours or overnight. To serve, cut into ½-inch slices.

Makes 4 to 6 servings

Country Style Paté in French Bread

Dijon Pesto & Cheese

Preparation Time: 30 minutes
Total Time: 2½ hours

1/2 **cup chopped parsley**
1/3 **cup GREY POUPON® Dijon or**
   Country Dijon Mustard
1/4 **cup walnuts, chopped**
1/4 **cup grated Parmesan cheese**
2 **teaspoons dried basil leaves**
2 **cloves garlic, crushed**
3 **(3-ounce) packages cream**
   cheese, well chilled
   Assorted NABISCO® Crackers
   Roasted red peppers and basil
   leaves, for garnish

In electric blender container, blend parsley, mustard, walnuts, Parmesan cheese, basil and garlic; set aside.

Roll each square of cream cheese between 2 sheets of waxed paper to an 8×4-inch rectangle. Place 1 cheese rectangle in plastic wrap-lined 8½×4½×4½-inch loaf pan; top with half the parsley mixture. Repeat layers, ending with remaining cheese rectangle. Chill at least 2 hours. Remove from pan; slice and serve on crackers garnished with peppers and basil, if desired. ***Makes 32 servings***

Beef and Cheese Canapés

Preparation Time: 15 minutes
Microwave Cooking Time:
1 to 1½ minutes

8 **ounces cooked lean rare roast**
   beef, sliced 1/8 inch thick
2 **ounces Gorgonzola or blue**
   cheese
1 **tablespoon butter or**
   margarine, softened
2 **tablespoons sliced green**
   onion with tops
32 **Melba toast rounds or**
   shredded whole wheat
   wafers
3 **tablespoons Dijon-style**
   mustard*

Cut sliced roast beef into 1/4-inch strips. In small bowl, combine Gorgonzola and butter; stir in green onion. Spread each cracker with approximately 1/4 teaspoon Dijon-style mustard. Top each with an equal amount of beef strips and approximately 1/2 teaspoon cheese mixture.** Place 16 appetizers on microwave-safe platter. Microwave at HIGH 30 to 45 seconds or until cheese mixture is melted. Repeat with remaining appetizers. Serve immediately.

Makes 32 appetizers

*One-third cup chutney may be substituted for Dijon-style mustard. Spread each cracker with approximately 1/2 teaspoon chutney.

**Cheddar cheese spread may be substituted for cheese and butter mixture.

Favorite recipe from **National Live Stock & Meat Board**

Miniature Teriyaki Pork Kabobs

Try

Preparation Time: 10 minutes
Cooking Time: 5 minutes

1 **pound boneless pork loin, cut**
   into 4×1×1/2-inch strips
1 **(11-ounce) can mandarin**
   oranges, drained
1 **small green pepper, cut into**
   1×1/4×1/4-inch strips
1/4 **cup teriyaki sauce**
1 **tablespoon honey**
1 **tablespoon vinegar**
1/8 **teaspoon garlic powder**

Soak 24 bamboo skewers in cold water 20 to 30 minutes. Thread pork strips, accordion-style, with mandarin oranges onto skewers. Add green pepper strip to ends of each skewer.

For sauce, in small bowl combine teriyaki sauce, honey, vinegar and garlic powder; mix well. Brush sauce over kabobs. Broil 6 inches from heat source 5 to 6 minutes, turning and brushing with sauce occasionally until pork is cooked through. ***Makes 24 servings***

Favorite recipe from **National Pork Producers Council**

Souper Nachos

Souper Nachos

  ¼ **pound ground beef**
  2 **envelopes LIPTON® Tomato**
     Cup-a-Soup Instant Soup
  ½ **cup water**
  1 **teaspoon red wine vinegar**
  ½ **to 1 teaspoon chili powder**
     Tortilla chips (about 30)
  ¼ **cup chopped green onions**
     (optional)
  1 **cup shredded Monterey Jack**
     or Cheddar cheese (about
     3 ounces)

In small microwave-safe bowl, microwave ground beef at HIGH (Full Power) 2 minutes or until no longer pink; drain. Stir in instant tomato soup mix, water, vinegar and chili powder. Microwave at HIGH 1½ minutes or until thickened, stirring once. Arrange ½ of the tortilla chips in one layer on microwave-safe plate, then top with ½ of the ground beef mixture, onions and cheese; repeat layer. Microwave at HIGH 1½ minutes or until cheese is melted.

Makes 4 servings

Conventional Directions: Preheat oven to 375°. In small skillet, brown ground beef; drain. Stir in instant tomato soup mix, water, vinegar and chili powder. Cook, stirring frequently, 1 minute or until mixture thickens. Arrange as previously indicated on ovenproof plate or baking dish. Bake 10 minutes or until cheese is melted.

Baked Brie

  1 **wedge (16 ounces) of Brie**
     cheese
  ¼ **cup packed brown sugar**
  ¼ **cup broken nuts**
  2 **tablespoons brandy or**
     bourbon
     KEEBLER® Original or Low Salt
     Wheatables Crackers

Bring cheese to room temperature. Pierce top of cheese with fork and bake at 500°F for 5 minutes. Remove from oven and top with brown sugar, nuts and brandy. Bake 5 minutes longer and serve with Keebler® Wheatables Crackers.

Makes 6 to 8 servings

Sweet & Spicy Dipping Sauce

⅓ cup COCO LOPEZ® Cream of Coconut
⅓ cup BENNETT'S® Chili Sauce
1 tablespoon REALEMON® Lemon Juice from Concentrate
2 teaspoons soy sauce
1 teaspoon Worcestershire sauce
½ to 1 teaspoon prepared horseradish
½ teaspoon hot pepper sauce

In small bowl, combine ingredients; mix well. Cover; refrigerate 4 hours or overnight. Serve chilled or at room temperature with Coconut Shrimp. Refrigerate leftovers.

Makes about 3/4 cup

Coconut Shrimp with Sweet & Spicy Dipping Sauce

Savory Polenta Squares

*Preparation Time: 20 minutes
Cooking Time: 12 minutes plus standing time*

1 cup milk
½ cup cornmeal
2 tablespoons green onion slices
¼ teaspoon pepper
6 OSCAR MAYER® Bacon Slices, crisply cooked, crumbled
1 cup (4 ounces) VELVEETA® Shredded Pasteurized Process Cheese Food
2 eggs, beaten
2 tablespoons chopped fresh basil

• Preheat oven to 400°.

• Line 8- or 9-inch square baking pan with foil; grease foil.

• Bring milk to boil in small saucepan over medium heat. Gradually add cornmeal, stirring constantly with wire whisk. Cook 2 minutes, stirring constantly. Stir in green onions and pepper.

• Remove from heat, stir in bacon, ½ cup process cheese food, eggs and basil. Spread into pan.

• Bake 10 minutes. Sprinkle with remaining ½ cup process cheese food; continue baking 2 minutes. Let stand 10 minutes; cut into squares. Serve warm.

Makes 3 dozen

Coconut Shrimp

1 pound large raw shrimp, peeled and deveined with tails on (about 20)
½ cup COCO LOPEZ® Cream of Coconut
3 tablespoons cornstarch
1 tablespoon REALEMON® Lemon Juice from Concentrate
1 teaspoon Worcestershire sauce
Additional cornstarch
⅔ cup flaked coconut
½ cup fresh bread crumbs (1 slice)
Vegetable oil
Sweet & Spicy Dipping Sauce

In medium bowl, combine cream of coconut, *3 tablespoons* cornstarch, ReaLemon® brand and Worcestershire; mix until smooth. Coat shrimp with cornstarch. Dip into cream of coconut batter; drain on wire rack. Coat with flaked coconut then bread crumbs. Place on baking sheet. Cover; refrigerate 1 hour or overnight. Into deep hot oil (375°), drop shrimp, 1 at a time; fry a few shrimp at a time until golden brown. Drain on paper towels. Serve with Sweet & Spicy Dipping Sauce. Refrigerate leftovers.

Makes about 20 appetizers

Tip: Recipe can be doubled. If using medium shrimp, use 1⅔ cups flaked coconut and 1 cup fresh bread crumbs.

Torta California

*Preparation Time: 15 minutes
plus refrigerating*

2 packages (8 ounces each)
   PHILADELPHIA BRAND® Cream
   Cheese, softened
1 package (8 ounces) goat
   cheese
1 to 2 garlic cloves
2 tablespoons olive oil
1 teaspoon dried thyme leaves,
   crushed
3 tablespoons prepared pesto,
   well drained
1/3 cup roasted red peppers,
   drained, chopped

- Line 1-quart souffle dish or loaf pan with plastic wrap.

- Place cream cheese, goat cheese and garlic in food processor container fitted with steel blade or blender container; process until well blended. Add oil and thyme; blend well.

- Place one third of cheese mixture in souffle dish; cover with pesto, half of remaining cheese mixture and peppers. Top with remaining cheese mixture. Cover. Refrigerate.

- Unmold; remove plastic wrap. Smooth sides. Garnish with fresh herbs and additional red pepper, if desired. Serve with assorted crackers or French bread.

Makes 3 cups

Torta California

Party Hero

- 3/4 pound creamy coleslaw
- 1/3 cup bottled salad dressing (Thousand Island, Creamy Italian or Creamy Blue Cheese)
- 1 (8-inch) round loaf of bread (French, Italian, sourdough or rye), about 1 1/2 pounds
- 1/2 pound cooked turkey, sliced
- 1/2 pound cooked ham, sliced
- 1/4 pound Cheddar, Muenster or Swiss cheese, sliced

Drain excess liquid from coleslaw; add 2 tablespoons bottled dressing to coleslaw, mixing well. Cut a thin slice from top of bread; spread cut surface of slice with some of the bottled dressing. Hollow out bread, leaving about 1/2-inch-thick bread shell. Line bread shell with leaf lettuce; brush with remaining bottled dressing. Press turkey onto bottom; cover with half of coleslaw mixture. Repeat with ham, remaining coleslaw mixture and cheese. Garnish with lettuce; cover with top bread slice. Place 6 to 8 long wooden picks into sandwich to secure. Chill no longer than 4 to 6 hours before serving. To serve, cut between picks to form 6 to 8 wedge-shaped sandwiches.

Makes 6 to 8 sandwiches

Party Hero

Chicken Cheese Ball

- 1 (8-ounce) package cream cheese, softened
- 1/2 cup finely chopped cooked chicken
- 1 (2-ounce) jar pimiento, drained and chopped
- 1 teaspoon WYLER'S® or STEERO® Chicken-Flavor Instant Bouillon
- 1/2 cup chopped walnuts

In small bowl, combine all ingredients except nuts; mix well. Chill. Shape into ball; roll in nuts to coat. Chill. Serve with crackers or fresh vegetables. Refrigerate leftovers.   **Makes 1 cheese ball**

Savory Walnut Risotto

- 2 cups sliced mushrooms
- 1/4 cup butter or margarine
- 1 clove garlic, minced
- 1 small onion, minced
- 1 cup short-grain rice (arborio rice, if available)
- 1/2 apple, finely chopped
- 1 3/4 cups (14 1/2-ounce can) chicken or beef broth
- 3/4 cup chopped walnuts
- 1/2 cup freshly grated Parmesan cheese
- 3 tablespoons minced parsley
- 1 pound cooked, shelled shrimp (optional)

Combine mushrooms, butter, garlic and onion in 3-quart glass casserole. Microwave on HIGH 4 to 5 minutes or until onion is transparent, stirring once. Stir in rice and apple; set aside. In 4-cup glass measure, microwave broth on HIGH 3 minutes; stir into rice mixture. Cover tightly and microwave on HIGH 5 minutes. Rotate dish 1/4 turn. Cook on MEDIUM (50% power) an additional 7 to 10 minutes or until liquid is absorbed. Stir in walnuts, cheese, parsley and shrimp, if desired. Cover and let stand 5 to 10 minutes.

Makes 4 to 6 servings

Favorite recipe from **Walnut Marketing Board**

Piña Colada Brie

Preparation Time: 5 minutes
Cooking Time: 15 minutes

1 (1-pound) round Brie cheese
1 can (8 ounces) DOLE® Crushed
   Pineapple in Syrup, drained*
3 tablespoons honey roasted
   peanuts
2 tablespoons brown sugar
2 tablespoons flaked coconut
French bread or crackers

- Place Brie on ovenproof serving platter.

- Combine drained pineapple, peanuts and sugar in small saucepan. Cook until thoroughly heated. Spoon mixture over cheese.

- Bake in 400°F oven 8 to 10 minutes or until cheese is softened. Sprinkle coconut over pineapple topping and continue to bake just until coconut is lightly toasted. Serve with French bread or crackers.

Makes 6 servings

*Use pineapple packed in juice if desired.

Marinated Cheese Cubes

1 pound mozzarella cheese,
   cubed
1 red onion, sliced
1 green bell pepper, cut into
   chunks
½ cup light Italian salad dressing
⅓ cup red wine vinegar
1 tablespoon DURKEE® Gourmet
   Basil Leaves
¼ teaspoon DURKEE® Gourmet
   Garlic Powder
¼ teaspoon DURKEE® Gourmet
   Ground Black Pepper

Combine cheese, onion and bell pepper in medium bowl. Add remaining ingredients and toss lightly to coat cheese. Cover; refrigerate 1 hour or overnight. Serve on a lettuce leaf as an appetizer salad, if des

Festive Pepper Medley à la Grecque

Festive Pepper Medley à la Grecque

1 green bell pepper, cut into thin
   strips
1 yellow bell pepper, cut into
   thin strips
1 red bell pepper, cut into thin
   strips
3 tablespoons olive or
   vegetable oil
2 teaspoons balsamic or red
   wine vinegar
1 tablespoon water
1 tablespoon chopped fresh
   oregano *or* 1 teaspoon dried
   oregano
   Salt and black pepper, to taste
¾ cup chopped walnuts
¼ cup olives (Greek or Nicoise)
¼ cup crumbled feta cheese
   (optional)

Arrange bell peppers on microwave-safe serving platter. In small bowl, combine oil, vinegar, water, oregano, salt and black pepper; pour over bell peppers. Sprinkle with walnuts. Microwave on HIGH 5 minutes or until peppers are cooked. Top with olives and cheese. Serve warm or at room temperature. Garnish with radicchio or spinach leaves, if desired.

Makes 4 to 6 servings

Favorite recipe from **Walnut Marketing Board**

Salmon Cucumber Mousse

Salmon Cucumber Mousse

*Preparation Time: 15 minutes
plus refrigerating*

**2 envelopes unflavored gelatin
1 cup cold water
2 tablespoons lemon juice
2 containers (8 ounces each)
    PHILADELPHIA BRAND® Soft
    Cream Cheese with Smoked
    Salmon
1 small cucumber, peeled, finely
    chopped**

- Soften gelatin in water; stir over
  low heat until dissolved. Stir in
  lemon juice.

- Stir cream cheese, gelatin mixture
  and cucumber in small bowl until
  well blended. Pour into 1-quart
  mold.

- Chill until firm. Unmold onto
  serving platter. Serve with melba
  toast rounds.   ***Makes 3 cups***

Fried Jack
Hors d'Oeuvres

**1½ pounds Monterey Jack cheese
    (7x3-inch block)
30 cloves fresh garlic
4 cups peanut or vegetable oil
    (more as needed)
1 tablespoon Italian seasoning
3 eggs, beaten
2 cups all-purpose flour
3 cups French bread crumbs*
3 tablespoons chopped fresh
    parsley
1 small jar marinara sauce
    (optional)**

Slice cheese into 30 slices, each
about ¼ inch thick. Peel garlic and
slice each clove lengthwise into
about 6 ovals. Heat oil in deep,
heavy saucepan over medium low
heat. Add garlic ovals and simmer
5 to 7 minutes, being careful not to
burn or brown cloves. Remove slices
as they float to surface and are light
brown in color. Drain on paper
towel. Reserve oil for cheese.

Mince garlic and mix with Italian
seasoning. Spread half the cheese
slices evenly with garlic mixture.
Press remaining cheese slices on
top to make 15 bars. Cut each bar
into 3 pieces. Dip into beaten egg,
then into flour. Dip flour-coated
pieces into egg again, then into
bread crumbs mixed with parsley.
(Be sure to cover sides.) Reheat oil to
medium-high and fry cheese sticks
in oil a few pieces at a time until
lightly browned, about 2 minutes.
(Skim particles from oil as they
accumulate.) Drain cheese on
paper towels and keep warm until
all are fried. Serve with toothpicks
and sauce for dipping, if desired.
            Makes about 45 pieces

*Use day-old bread and prepare
crumbs in food processor. Dry
packaged crumbs may be used
but are not as attractive when fried.

Favorite recipe from **Fresh Garlic
Association**

Mexican Appetizer Cheesecake

2 teaspoons WYLER'S® or STEERO®
    Chicken-Flavor Instant
    Bouillon
1/2 cup *hot* water
3 (8-ounce) packages cream
    cheese, softened
1 1/2 teaspoons chili powder
1/2 to 1 teaspoon hot pepper
    sauce
2 eggs
1 cup finely chopped cooked
    chicken
1 (4-ounce) can chopped green
    chilies, *well drained*
    Salsa, shredded cheese and
    sliced green onions
    LA FAMOUS® Tortilla Chips

Preheat oven to 325°. Dissolve bouillon in water; set aside. In large mixer bowl, beat cream cheese, chili powder and hot pepper sauce until smooth. Add eggs; mix well. Add bouillon liquid, beating until smooth. Stir in chicken and chilies. Pour into 9-inch springform pan. Bake 30 minutes or until set; cool 15 minutes. Carefully run knife around edge of pan; remove side of pan. Top with salsa, cheese and green onions. Serve warm or chilled with tortilla chips. Refrigerate leftovers.

Makes 8 to 10 servings

Walnut and Celery Appetizer Pie

1 egg yolk
1 KEEBLER® Ready-Crust® Graham
    Cracker Pie Crust
1 (8-ounce) package cream
    cheese, softened
1 (3-ounce) package cream
    cheese, softened
1 cup sour cream, divided
2 eggs
1 tablespoon all-purpose flour
1/4 teaspoon celery salt
    Freshly ground black pepper
    to taste
1 1/2 cups coarsely chopped
    walnuts, divided
1/2 cup chopped celery
1 teaspoon Worcestershire sauce

Beat egg yolk and brush on crust. Bake in preheated 350°F oven 5 minutes. Set aside. In large mixing bowl, beat cream cheese, 1/2 cup sour cream, eggs, flour, celery salt and pepper until smooth. Fold in 3/4 cup walnuts, celery and Worcestershire. Spoon filling into prepared pie crust and bake 50 minutes or until set. Remove from oven and spread remaining 1/2 cup sour cream over top of pie. Sprinkle remaining 3/4 cup chopped walnuts over sour cream. Cool to room temperature and refrigerate at least 4 hours or overnight. Serve with assorted fresh fruits.

Makes 16 servings

Vegetable 'n Herb Topper

4 ounces light cream cheese,
    softened
1/4 cup shredded reduced-fat
    Cheddar cheese (about
    1 ounce)
1/2 teaspoon chopped dried
    chives
1/2 teaspoon dried thyme leaves
30 AMERICAN CLASSIC® Golden
    Sesame Crackers
30 vegetable pieces, blanched
    (broccoli flowerets,
    asparagus tips, pepper strips,
    carrot slices)

In bowl, blend cheeses and herbs. Top each cracker with 1 teaspoon cheese mixture and 1 vegetable piece.

Place 6 topped crackers in a circle on microwavable plate. Microwave at HIGH (100% power) for 15 to 25 seconds or until cheese softens. Repeat with remaining topped crackers. Serve immediately.

Makes 30 appetizers

Swedish Cocktail Meatballs

1/2 pound lean ground beef
1/2 pound ground seasoned sausage
1/2 cup fine dry bread crumbs (unseasoned)
1 egg
1/2 teaspoon salt, divided
1/8 teaspoon pepper
1/8 teaspoon ground nutmeg
2 tablespoons BUTTER FLAVOR CRISCO®, divided
1/4 cup finely chopped onion
1/4 cup finely chopped celery
2 tablespoons all-purpose flour
1 cup milk
2 tablespoons snipped fresh parsley
Dash ground nutmeg
1/2 cup dairy sour cream

In large mixing bowl combine beef, sausage, bread crumbs, egg, 1/4 teaspoon salt, pepper and 1/8 teaspoon nutmeg. Mix well. Set aside.

In large skillet melt 1 tablespoon Butter Flavor Crisco®. Add onion and celery. Cook and stir over medium heat until tender. Stir into meat mixture.

Shape by rounded teaspoonfuls into balls. In large skillet melt remaining 1 tablespoon Butter Flavor Crisco®. Add meatballs; cook over medium heat until firm and golden brown. Remove and drain on paper towels.

Stir flour into drippings in skillet. Blend in milk, parsley, remaining 1/4 teaspoon salt and dash nutmeg. Cook and stir over medium heat until mixture thickens. Remove from heat. Blend in sour cream. Add meatballs, stirring to coat. Cook until heated through. *Do not boil.* Serve with cocktail picks.

Makes about 36 appetizers

Cajun Ham Mini Sandwiches

*Preparation/Marinating Time:
40 minutes
Assembly/Microwave Cooking Time:
18 minutes*

1 can (12 ounces) light beer
1 small onion, chopped
1 clove garlic, quartered
1 bay leaf
1 cinnamon stick
4 whole cloves
1/2 teaspoon crushed red pepper
1/4 teaspoon dried thyme leaves
16 slices (12 ounces) cooked smoked lean ham
Peach Mustard Spread (recipe follows)
16 cocktail-size buns, split
4 slices (3 ounces) Swiss cheese, quartered

Combine beer and seasonings in 4-cup microwave-safe glass measure. Cover with plastic wrap, venting corner. Microwave at HIGH 5 minutes. Cool; strain into bowl. (May be made up to 24 hours ahead.) Add ham slices; cover and marinate 30 minutes. Drain marinade. Meanwhile, spread scant teaspoonful of Peach Mustard Spread on cut side of each bun. Place cheese square on bottom. Top with folded ham slice and top half of bun. Place 4 sandwiches on microwave-safe plate; cover with paper towel and microwave at HIGH 45 seconds. Repeat with remaining sandwiches.

Makes 16 sandwiches

Peach Mustard Spread
Combine 1/3 cup peach fruit spread and 2 teaspoons horseradish or Dijon-style mustard.

Favorite recipe from **National Live Stock & Meat Board**

Cocktail Party Tray

- 1 pound large raw shrimp, peeled and deveined
- 1 pound chicken wing drumettes
- 1 pound skinned boneless chicken breasts, cut into strips
- 1½ cups BENNETT'S® Chili or Hot Seafood Sauce
- 1 (12-ounce) jar BENNETT'S® Cocktail Sauce

In 3 separate plastic bags, combine shrimp, chicken wings and chicken strips each with *½ cup* chili or hot seafood sauce. Marinate in refrigerator a few hours or overnight. Remove from sauce. Broil or grill until done, basting frequently with sauce. Serve with cocktail sauce. Refrigerate leftovers. ***Makes 12 servings***

Tip: Shrimp can be arranged on skewers with water chestnuts or tomatillo wedges before broiling.

Meatball Nibbles

- 1 pound ground beef
- 2 envelopes LIPTON® Onion Cup-a-Soup Instant Soup
- 1 egg
- ⅓ cup plain dry bread crumbs
- ¼ cup ketchup
- 2 tablespoons finely chopped parsley

In medium bowl, combine all ingredients. Shape into 1-inch meatballs; divide into three batches. Place one batch on 9-inch microwave-safe round shallow dish; cover with wax paper. Microwave at HIGH (Full Power) 4 minutes or until done. Repeat with remaining batches. Serve, if desired, with assorted mustards or tomato sauce.

Makes about 48 meatballs

Conventional Directions: Preheat oven to 375°. Shape meatballs as above. In shallow baking pan, arrange meatballs and bake 18 minutes or until done. Serve as above.

Cocktail Party Tray

South-of-the-Border Torte

teaspoon garlic powder. In small bowl, stir together remaining *1 cup* sour cream, the green onion and remaining *1/2 teaspoon each* chili powder and oregano.

Warm tortillas according to package directions. Place 1 tortilla on large serving dish; top with refried bean mixture. Top with second tortilla; spread with avocado mixture. Top with third tortilla; spoon on tomato mixture. Top with fourth tortilla; spread with sour cream mixture. Sprinkle with remaining *1/4 cup* cheese. Garnish with ripe olives, additional chopped tomatoes and green onion, if desired. To serve, cut into wedges.

Makes 12 servings

South-of-the-Border Torte

    1 can (16 ounces) refried beans
1 1/4 cups shredded Cheddar
      cheese
1 1/2 teaspoons DURKEE® Gourmet
      Garlic Powder
1 1/2 teaspoons DURKEE® Gourmet
      Oregano
   1/2 teaspoon DURKEE® Gourmet
      Ground Red Pepper
    1 ripe avocado, peeled and
      mashed
1 1/4 cups sour cream
   1/2 teaspoon lemon juice
    2 teaspoons chili powder
    1 cup chopped tomatoes
    1 can (4 ounces) chopped
      green chilies, drained
   1/3 cup chopped green onion
    4 (8- to 10-inch) flour tortillas

In medium saucepan, combine refried beans, *1 cup* cheese, *1 teaspoon each* garlic powder and oregano and *1/4 teaspoon* ground red pepper. Simmer over low heat until heated through. In small bowl, combine avocado, *1/4 cup* sour cream, lemon juice, *1/2 teaspoon* chili powder and remaining *1/4 teaspoon* ground red pepper. In another small bowl, combine tomatoes, green chilies, *1 teaspoon* chili powder and remaining *1/2*

Appetizer Quiche Squares

Pastry
1 1/4 cups all-purpose flour
   1/2 teaspoon salt
   1/2 cup BUTTER FLAVOR CRISCO®
    2 to 3 tablespoons water

Filling
    3 eggs, slightly beaten
    1 can (12 ounces) evaporated
      milk
    2 tablespoons all-purpose flour
   1/2 teaspoon Worcestershire sauce
   1/4 teaspoon salt
   1/8 teaspoon garlic powder
    1 can (6 1/2 ounces) tiny shrimp,
      drained
    1 cup shredded Cheddar
      cheese
   1/2 cup grated carrot
   1/4 cup chopped onion

For pastry, preheat oven to 325°F. In medium bowl, combine 1 1/4 cups flour and 1/2 teaspoon salt. Cut in Butter Flavor Crisco® using pastry blender or 2 knives to form coarse crumbs. Add water, 1 tablespoon at a time, mixing with fork until particles are moistened and cling together. Form dough into ball. Roll into a 10-inch square on lightly floured board. Place dough in 9-inch square baking pan. Press up around edges of pan to form 1-inch rim. Bake at 325°F for 10 minutes. Set aside.

For filling, in large bowl, blend eggs, evaporated milk, 2 tablespoons flour, Worcestershire sauce, ¼ teaspoon salt and garlic powder. Stir in shrimp, cheese, carrot and onion. Pour into partially baked pastry. Bake at 325°F for 30 to 35 minutes or until knife inserted in center comes out clean. Cut into 20 squares. ***Makes 20 appetizers***

Cream Puff Appetizers

Cream Puffs
½ cup water
¼ cup BUTTER FLAVOR CRISCO®
½ cup all-purpose flour
⅛ teaspoon salt
2 eggs

Chicken Filling
2 cups finely chopped cooked chicken
⅔ cup mayonnaise or salad dressing
½ cup finely chopped celery
⅓ cup finely chopped almonds
1 hard cooked egg, finely chopped
1½ teaspoons lemon juice
¾ teaspoon salt
¼ teaspoon pepper

For cream puffs, preheat oven to 400°F. In medium saucepan combine water and Butter Flavor Crisco®. Heat to rolling boil. Add flour and salt, stirring until mixture forms a ball. Continue to cook and stir 1 minute. Remove from heat. Add eggs all at once, beating until smooth.

Drop by ½ teaspoonfuls at least 1½ inches apart onto ungreased baking sheet. Bake at 400°F for 20 to 30 minutes or until golden brown. Cool. Meanwhile, prepare chicken filling.

For chicken filling, in medium bowl combine all ingredients. Mix thoroughly. Cover and refrigerate at least 30 minutes.

To fill, cut off tops of cooled cream puffs. Remove excess dough from inside. Fill with chicken filling. Replace tops.
Makes about 24 appetizers

Pork and Crab Dumplings

Preparation Time: 30 minutes
Cooking Time: 18 minutes

1 cup finely chopped cooked pork tenderloin
1 (6-ounce) can crab meat, drained and flaked
¼ cup finely chopped onion
2 tablespoons finely chopped water chestnuts
2 teaspoons soy sauce
¼ teaspoon salt
⅛ teaspoon black pepper
1 (3-ounce) package cream cheese, softened
About 20 wonton wrappers
4 tablespoons vegetable oil, divided
1 cup water
Chinese mustard
Soy sauce

In large bowl combine pork, crab, onion, water chestnuts, 2 teaspoons soy sauce, salt and pepper; mix well. Stir in cream cheese; mix well and set aside.

Cut wonton wrappers into 4-inch circles using cookie cutter. (Keep wonton wrappers covered with dry cloth when not working with wrappers). Spoon about 1 tablespoon filling in center of one round. Fold wrapper in half across filling; moisten and pinch edges to seal. Set pinched edge upright and press gently to flatten bottom. Transfer to baking sheet and cover with dry cloth. Repeat with remaining rounds and filling.

In large skillet heat 2 tablespoons oil. Carefully place half the dumplings in skillet (do not let dumplings touch). Cook over medium heat 1 minute or until bottoms are browned. Reduce heat; carefully add ½ cup water to skillet. Cover and simmer 10 minutes. Uncover and cook 3 to 5 minutes or until water evaporates. (Add more oil, if necessary). Cook uncovered 1 minute. Transfer dumplings to baking sheet. Place in 250°F oven to keep warm. Repeat with remaining dumplings, oil and water. Serve with Chinese mustard and soy sauce for dipping. ***Makes 20 appetizers***

Favorite recipe from **National Pork Producers Council**

Sparkling White Sangria

Preparation Time: 15 minutes, plus standing and chilling

1 cup KARO® Light Corn Syrup
1 orange, sliced
1 lemon, sliced
1 lime, sliced
1/2 cup orange-flavored liqueur
1 bottle (750 ml) dry white wine
2 tablespoons lemon juice
1 bottle (12 ounces) club soda or seltzer, chilled
Additional fresh fruit (optional)

In large pitcher combine corn syrup, orange, lemon and lime slices and liqueur. Let stand 20 to 30 minutes, stirring occasionally. Stir in wine and lemon juice. Refrigerate. Just before serving, add soda and ice cubes. If desired, garnish with additional fruit.

Makes about 6 (8-ounce) servings

Chi Chi Punch

Preparation Time: 10 minutes

6 cups DOLE® Pineapple Orange Juice, chilled
1 can (15 ounces) cream of coconut
3 cups vodka
1 quart lemon-lime soda
Cracked ice
1 orange, thinly sliced
Mint sprigs

- Blend 1 cup pineapple orange juice and cream of coconut in blender. Add to punch bowl with remaining pineapple orange juice. Stir in vodka.
- Just before serving, add lemon-lime soda and ice. Garnish with orange slices and mint sprigs.

Makes 30 (4-ounce) servings

Bloody Mary Mix

1 quart vegetable juice cocktail
2 tablespoons HEINZ® Worcestershire Sauce
1 tablespoon fresh lime or lemon juice
1/4 teaspoon granulated sugar
1/4 teaspoon pepper
1/4 teaspoon hot pepper sauce
1/8 teaspoon garlic powder

In pitcher, thoroughly combine vegetable juice, Worcestershire sauce, lime juice, sugar, pepper, hot pepper sauce and garlic powder; cover and chill. Serve over ice. Garnish with celery stalks and lime wedges, if desired.

Makes about 1 quart

Note: To prepare Bloody Mary Cocktail, add 3 or 4 parts Bloody Mary Mix to 1 part vodka.

Sparkling White Sangria

Daiquiri in Paradise

2 ripe, medium DOLE® Bananas, peeled
2 cups crushed ice
²/₃ cup frozen DOLE® Pine-Passion-Banana Juice concentrate, thawed
½ cup water
¼ cup dark or light rum
¼ cup orange liqueur

• Combine all ingredients in blender; puree until slushy. Serve in stemmed glasses. Garnish as desired. **Makes 6 servings**

Left: Sunlight Sipper
Right: Daiquiri in Paradise

Sunlight Sipper

4 cups DOLE® Pine-Passion-Banana Juice
2 tablespoons peach schnapps
2 tablespoons light rum
2 tablespoons orange liqueur
Cracked ice

• Combine all liquid ingredients. Serve over cracked ice in glasses. Garnish as desired.
Makes 6 servings

Cranberry Pineapple Smoothie

Preparation Time: 10 minutes

2 cups Cranberry Pineapple Smoothie Base (recipe follows)
1 large ripe banana (optional)
4 cups ice cubes
Orange peel and mint leaves (optional)

Prepare Cranberry Pineapple Smoothie Base. In blender combine 2 cups Smoothie Base and banana; process until smooth. With blender running, add ice cubes, several at a time. Process until thick and smooth. If desired, garnish with orange peel and mint leaves.
Makes about 6 (6-ounce) servings

Cranberry Pineapple Smoothie Base

1 cup KARO® Light Corn Syrup
1 can (16 ounces) whole berry cranberry sauce
1 can (8 ounces) crushed pineapple in unsweetened juice, undrained

In blender combine ingredients; process until smooth. Store covered in refrigerator up to 1 week.
Makes 4 cups base

Hot Holiday Punch

1 cup granulated sugar
½ cup packed brown sugar
4 cups apple cider
1 cinnamon stick
12 whole cloves
2 cups Florida Grapefruit Juice
2 cups Florida Orange Juice
Orange slices
Maraschino cherry halves
(optional)
Whole cloves (optional)

Combine sugars and apple cider in large saucepan. Heat over medium heat, stirring until sugars dissolve. Add cinnamon stick and cloves. Bring to a boil over medium heat. Reduce heat to low; simmer 5 minutes. Add grapefruit and orange juice. Heat, but do not boil. Strain into heatproof punch bowl. Garnish with orange slices decorated with maraschino cherry halves and whole cloves. Serve in heatproof punch cups.

Makes 8 (8-ounce) servings

Favorite recipe from **Florida Department of Citrus**

Kahlúa® Chi Chi

4 cups finely crushed ice
16 ounces (2 cups) pineapple juice
8 ounces (1 cup) KAHLÚA®
8 ounces (1 cup) coconut milk or cream of coconut
6 ounces (⅔ cup) vodka

In blender, combine half of all ingredients and blend until smooth. Pour into tall glasses. Repeat with remaining ingredients. Garnish each glass with mint sprig, if desired.

Makes 8 servings

Hot Holiday Punch

Zesty Punch Sipper

Kahlúa® Toasted Almond

8 ounces (1 cup) KAHLÚA®
4 ounces (½ cup) amaretto
liqueur
Cream or milk

For each serving, pour 1 ounce Kahlúa® and ½ ounce amaretto liqueur over ice in tall glass. Fill with cream; stir.   ***Makes 8 servings***

Lime Party Punch

Preparation Time: 10 minutes

1 package (4-serving size)
JELL-O® Brand Gelatin, Lime
Flavor
1 package (4-serving size)
JELL-O® Brand Gelatin, Lemon
Flavor
2 cups boiling water
1 bottle (1 liter) club soda, lemon
soda or lemon-lime
carbonated beverage,
chilled
1 cup white wine (optional)
1 orange, lemon or lime, thinly
sliced
Ice cubes (optional)

Dissolve gelatins in boiling water; cool. (Keep at room temperature until ready to serve.) Stir in club soda, wine and orange slices just before serving. Serve over ice, if desired.

Makes 8 cups or 16 servings

Zesty Punch Sipper

2 bottles (32 ounces each)
ginger ale, chilled
6 cups DOLE® Pineapple Orange
Juice, chilled
1 can (6 ounces) frozen
lemonade concentrate,
thawed
1 DOLE® Orange, thinly sliced for
garnish, optional
1 lime, thinly sliced for garnish,
optional

• Combine all ingredients in large punch bowl or two large pitchers.
Makes 20 servings

Sangrita

1 can (12 ounces) tomato juice
1½ cups orange juice
¼ cup lime or lemon juice
1 tablespoon finely minced
    onion
⅛ teaspoon salt
¼ teaspoon hot pepper sauce
    Ice cubes
4 small celery stalks with leafy
    tops

Combine juices, onion, salt and hot
pepper sauce in 1-quart container
with tight-fitting lid. Cover;
refrigerate 2 hours for flavors to
blend. Pour into ice-filled tumblers.
Add celery stalk to each glass for
stirrer.   **Makes 4 servings**

Sangrita

Piña Colada Smoothie

Preparation Time: 10 minutes

½ cup Piña Colada Smoothie
    Base (recipe follows)
1 small ripe banana
1 cup pineapple juice
4 cups ice cubes
¾ cup rum (optional)
    Fresh fruit (optional)

Prepare Piña Colada Smoothie
Base. In blender combine ½ cup
Smoothie Base with banana and
pineapple juice; process until
smooth. With blender running, add
ice cubes, several at a time, then
rum. Process until thick and smooth.
If desired, garnish with fresh fruit.
    Makes about 6 (6-ounce) servings

Piña Colada Smoothie Base

1 cup KARO® Light Corn Syrup
1 can (8 ounces) crushed
    pineapple in unsweetened
    juice, undrained
1 can (15 ounces) cream of
    coconut
¼ cup lime juice

In blender combine ingredients;
process until smooth. Store covered
in refrigerator up to 1 week.
    Makes 3½ cups base

Top: Strawberry Margarita
Bottom: Frozen Margarita

Strawberry Margaritas

1 (10-ounce) package frozen
   strawberries in syrup,
   partially thawed
1/4 cup REALIME® Lime Juice from
   Concentrate
1/4 cup tequila
1/4 cup confectioners' sugar
2 tablespoons triple sec or other
   orange-flavored liqueur
3 cups ice cubes

In blender container, combine all
ingredients except ice; blend well.
Gradually add ice, blending until
smooth. Serve immediately.

Makes about 1 quart

Kahlúa® Aggravation

8 ounces (1 cup) KAHLÚA®
12 ounces (1 1/2 cups) scotch
   Cream

For each serving, pour 1 ounce
Kahlúa® and 1 1/2 ounces scotch over
ice in tall glass. Fill with cream; stir.

Makes 8 servings

Peachy Beach Daiquiris

3 fresh California peaches,
   quartered
3 1/2 ounces dark rum
1/3 cup lime juice
1/3 cup sugar
10 ice cubes
4 fresh California peach slices
   (optional garnish)
4 lime slices (optional garnish)

In blender or food processor,
combine all ingredients except ice
and peach and lime slices. Blend
until smooth. Gradually add ice.
Blend until smooth. Serve
immediately. Garnish with peach
and lime slices, if desired.

Makes 4 servings

Tip: For non-alcoholic version,
substitute pineapple juice for rum
and decrease sugar to 3
tablespoons.

Favorite recipe from **California Tree Fruit
Agreement**

Frozen Margaritas

1/2 cup tequila
1/3 cup REALIME® Lime Juice from
   Concentrate
1/4 cup triple sec or other orange-
   flavored liqueur
1 cup confectioners' sugar
4 cups ice cubes

In blender container, combine all
ingredients except ice; blend well.
Gradually add ice, blending until
smooth. Serve immediately.

Makes about 1 quart

Mai Tai

3 cups DOLE® Pineapple Juice
1/4 cup light rum
1/4 cup dark rum
1/4 cup orange liqueur
1/4 cup frozen limeade
   concentrate, thawed
   Cracked ice

• Combine liquid ingredients. Serve
   over cracked ice in stemmed
   glasses. Garnish as desired.

Makes 6 servings

Strawberry Ginger Punch

Cranberry-Orange Cooler

Preparation Time: 5 minutes

- 1 package (4-serving size)
  JELL-O® Brand Gelatin,
  Orange Flavor
- 1 cup boiling water
- 2½ cups cranberry juice, chilled
  Ice cubes (optional)
  Orange slices (optional)

Dissolve gelatin in boiling water.
Add cranberry juice. Pour over ice
cubes in tall glasses and garnish
with orange slices, if desired.
Makes about 3½ cups or 4 servings

Mai Tai Slush

- 1½ cups DOLE® Pineapple Juice
- 1 pint lemon or lime sherbet
- 1 cup crushed ice
- ¼ cup rum
- 2 tablespoons orange liqueur
  Lime slices

- Combine all ingredients, except
  lime slices, in blender. Process until
  well blended. Pour into glasses.
  Garnish with lime slices.
  Makes 4 to 6 servings

Strawberry Ginger Punch

Preparation Time: 10 minutes

- 1 package (4-serving size)
  JELL-O® Brand Gelatin,
  Strawberry Flavor
- ¼ cup sugar
- 1½ cups boiling water
- 2½ cups cold water
- 1 package (10 ounces) BIRDS
  EYE® Quick Thaw Strawberries
- 1 can (6 ounces) frozen
  concentrated lemonade or
  limeade
- 1 bottle (1 liter) ginger ale,
  chilled
  Mint leaves
  Ice cubes (optional)

Dissolve gelatin and sugar in boiling
water. Add cold water, strawberries
and concentrate; stir until
strawberries and concentrate are
thawed. Chill until ready to serve.
Stir in ginger ale and mint. Serve
over ice, if desired.
Makes 10 cups or 20 servings

Left: Mai Tai; Right: Mai Tai Slush

Sangria Blush

1 cup orange juice
1/2 cup sugar
1 bottle (1.5 liters) white zinfandel wine
1/4 cup lime or lemon juice
1 orange, thinly sliced and seeded
1 lime, thinly sliced and seeded
16 to 20 ice cubes

Combine orange juice and sugar in small pan. Cook over medium heat, stirring occasionally, until sugar is dissolved. Pour into 2-quart container with tight-fitting lid. Add wine, lime juice and sliced fruits. Cover; refrigerate 2 hours for flavors to blend. Place ice cubes in small punch bowl or large pitcher. Pour wine mixture over ice.

Makes 8 servings

Sugar-Peach Champagne Cocktail

2 fresh California peaches, sliced
1/4 cup sugar
1 bottle (750 ml) pink Champagne

Roll peach slices in sugar and place 2 or 3 slices in each of 4 glasses. Fill with Champagne.

Makes 4 servings

Tip: Turn this into a fruit starter for Sunday brunch by filling a Champagne glass with fruit slices. Top with Champagne.

Favorite recipe from **California Tree Fruit Agreement**

Chi Chi

4 ounces or 1/2 cup DOLE® Pineapple Juice
3 ounces vodka
2 ounces cream of coconut
2 cups crushed ice

• Pour all ingredients into blender; blend at high speed briefly. Strain into glasses and serve.

Makes 2 servings

Lemony Light Cooler

3 cups white grape juice *or* 1 (750ml) bottle dry white wine, chilled
1/2 to 3/4 cup sugar
1/2 cup REALEMON® Lemon Juice from Concentrate
1 (32-ounce) bottle club soda, chilled
Strawberries, plum, peach or orange slices or other fresh fruit
Ice

In pitcher, combine grape juice, sugar and ReaLemon® brand; stir until sugar dissolves. Cover; chill. Just before serving, add club soda and fruit. Serve over ice.

Makes about 7 cups

Tip: Recipe can be doubled.

Peach 'n Cream Coladas

4 fresh California peaches, quartered
1 cup pineapple juice, chilled
1/2 cup cream of coconut, chilled
2 teaspoons rum extract
15 ice cubes
4 slices fresh California peaches

In blender or food processor, blend quartered peaches until smooth. Add remaining ingredients except peach slices and blend until slushy. Pour into glasses and decorate rim with peach slice. Serve immediately.

Makes 4 servings

Cocktail: Substitute 2 ounces light rum for rum extract.

Tip: Cream of coconut can be found in most liquor stores or in some grocery gourmet sections.

Favorite recipe from **California Tree Fruit Agreement**

Lemony Light Cooler

Bacon Appetizer Crescents

Preparation Time: 30 minutes
Cooking Time: 15 minutes

1 package (8 ounces)
   PHILADELPHIA BRAND® Cream
   Cheese, softened
8 OSCAR MAYER® Bacon Slices,
   crisply cooked, crumbled
1/3 cup (1 1/2 ounces) KRAFT® 100%
   Grated Parmesan Cheese
1/4 cup finely chopped onion
2 tablespoons chopped parsley
1 tablespoon milk
2 cans (8 ounces each)
   refrigerated crescent dinner
   rolls
1 egg, beaten
1 teaspoon cold water

- Heat oven to 375°F.

- Beat cream cheese, bacon, parmesan cheese, onion, parsley and milk in small mixing bowl at medium speed with electric mixer until well blended.

- Separate dough into eight rectangles; firmly press perforations together to seal. Spread each rectangle with 2 rounded measuring tablespoonfuls cream cheese mixture.

- Cut each rectangle in half diagonally; repeat with opposite corners. Cut in half crosswise to form six triangles. Roll up triangles, starting at short ends.

- Place on greased cookie sheet; brush with combined egg and water. Sprinkle with poppy seed, if desired.

- Bake 12 to 15 minutes or until golden brown. Serve immediately.
   Makes about 4 dozen

Spicy Southern Shrimp Kabobs

Preparation Time: 20 minutes
Cooking Time: 10 minutes

1 large DOLE® Fresh Pineapple
24 to 26 large shrimp, shelled
6 spicy Italian sausages, cut into
   1-inch pieces
1/2 medium DOLE® Red Bell
   Pepper, cut into chunks
1/2 medium DOLE® Green Bell
   Pepper, cut into chunks
1/4 cup margarine or butter,
   melted
3/4 teaspoon oregano, crumbled
3/4 teaspoon thyme, crumbled
1/2 teaspoon salt
1/4 teaspoon ground red pepper
1/4 teaspoon black pepper

- Twist crown from pineapple. Cut pineapple in half lengthwise. Cut fruit from shell with knife. Trim off core. Cut fruit into 24 chunks.

- Soak 12 to 14 (8-inch) wooden skewers in water 5 minutes.

- For each kabob, skewer 2 pineapple chunks, shrimp, sausage chunk and red or green bell pepper chunk. (Or arrange as desired to increase the number of appetizers.) Arrange skewers on rack in broiler pan coated with oil or cooking spray.

- Combine margarine and spices; brush over kabobs.

- Broil 6 inches from heat source 8 to 10 minutes, basting and turning occasionally until shrimp turn pink. Cool slightly before serving.
   Makes 12 kabobs

Bacon Appetizer Crescents

Dipper's Chicken Nuggets

Dipper's Chicken Nuggets

- 2 whole chicken breasts, split, skinned and boned
  Vegetable oil
- 1 egg
- 1/3 cup water
- 1/3 cup all-purpose flour
- 2 teaspoons sesame seeds
- 1 1/2 teaspoons salt
  Dipping Sauces (recipes follow)
  Red onion rings, for garnish

Cut chicken into 1-inch pieces. Heat 3 inches oil in large heavy saucepan over medium-high heat until oil reaches 375°F; adjust heat to maintain temperature. Meanwhile, beat egg and water in large bowl until well mixed. Add flour, sesame seeds and salt, stirring to form smooth batter. Dip chicken pieces into batter, draining off excess. Fry chicken, a few pieces at a time, in hot oil about 4 minutes or until golden brown. Drain on paper towels. Serve with Dipping Sauces; garnish with onion rings.

Makes 8 servings

Dipping Sauces

Nippy Pineapple Sauce

Mix 1 jar (12 ounces) pineapple preserves, 1/4 cup prepared mustard and 1/4 cup prepared horseradish in small saucepan. Cook and stir over low heat 5 minutes.

Dill Sauce

Combine 1/2 cup sour cream, 1/2 cup mayonnaise, 2 tablespoons finely chopped dill pickle and 1 teaspoon dill weed in small bowl. Cover; refrigerate 1 hour.

Royalty Sauce

Combine 1 cup ketchup, 6 tablespoons butter or margarine, 2 tablespoons vinegar, 1 tablespoon brown sugar and 1/2 teaspoon dry mustard in small saucepan. Cook and stir over low heat 5 minutes.

Favorite recipe from **National Broiler Council**

Clam 'n' Curry Roll-Ups

- 2 (6 1/2-ounce) cans SNOW'S® or DOXSEE® Minced Clams, drained
- 1/2 cup mayonnaise or salad dressing
- 1 tablespoon grated onion
- 1/4 to 1/2 teaspoon curry powder
- 8 slices white sandwich bread, crusts removed
  Melted margarine or butter
  Chopped parsley or toasted sesame seeds, optional

In bowl, combine clams, mayonnaise, onion and curry powder. Flatten each bread slice with rolling pin. Spread 2 tablespoons clam mixture on each bread slice; roll up. Brush with margarine. Wrap in plastic wrap; refrigerate or freeze. Before baking, roll in chopped parsley if desired. Preheat oven to 350°. Cut each roll into 4 pieces; place on rack in shallow baking pan. Bake 8 to 10 minutes or until golden brown. Serve immediately. Refrigerate leftovers.

Makes 32 appetizers

Antipasto-on-a-Stick

Preparation Time: 10 minutes

- 8 slices cooked lean beef (about 12 ounces), cut into 1-inch strips
- 16 pitted ripe olives
- 8 small cherry tomatoes
- 8 cubes provolone cheese (³/₄-inch)
- 8 marinated artichoke heart quarters, drained
- ¹/₂ cup Italian salad dressing
- 2 cups torn Bibb or Romaine lettuce (optional)

Roll up beef strips pinwheel fashion. Alternately arrange beef pinwheels, olives, cherry tomatoes, cheese cubes and artichoke hearts on eight 9-inch skewers. Place kabobs in shallow container; pour dressing over kabobs. Refrigerate several hours or overnight. To serve, arrange skewers on top of lettuce, if desired. Pour remaining dressing over all.

Makes 8 appetizers

Favorite recipe from **National Live Stock & Meat Board**

Deep-Fried Zucchini

- 1¹/₂ cups all-purpose flour, divided
- 2 tablespoons cornstarch
- ³/₄ teaspoon lemon pepper
- ¹/₂ teaspoon baking powder
- ¹/₂ teaspoon salt
- ¹/₄ teaspoon onion powder
- 1 cup milk
- 1 egg
- 1 pound fresh zucchini (about 3 medium)
  BUTTER FLAVOR CRISCO® for frying
  Grated Parmesan cheese

In medium bowl combine 1 cup flour, cornstarch, lemon pepper, baking powder, salt and onion powder. Stir in milk and egg; blend until smooth. Refrigerate at least 30 minutes.

Cut zucchini into ¹/₄-inch diagonal slices. Rinse and pat dry. Shake slices in remaining ¹/₂ cup flour to coat.

In deep-fat fryer or deep saucepan heat 2 to 3 inches Butter Flavor Crisco® to 375°F. Dip floured zucchini in chilled batter. Let excess drip back into bowl. Fry coated zucchini, a few at a time, in hot oil 4 to 4¹/₂ minutes or until golden brown, turning several times. Drain on paper towels. Serve immediately or keep warm in 175°F oven. Sprinkle with Parmesan cheese before serving.

Makes 4 to 5 dozen appetizers

Tip: To make a day ahead, prepare and fry as directed. Cool. Cover and refrigerate. Reheat in single layer on baking sheet in 425°F oven about 10 minutes or until hot. Sprinkle with Parmesan cheese.

Cheese Straws

- ¹/₂ cup unsalted butter, softened
- 1¹/₂ cups flour
- ¹/₂ teaspoon salt
- 1 package (4 ounces) SARGENTO® Fancy Shredded Swiss Cheese or Cheddar Cheese
- 2 tablespoons ice water

Cream butter in large bowl with electric mixer. Add flour and salt; beat 1 minute. Add cheese; beat 1 minute. Sprinkle with water; beat until dough begins to come together. Press into 5-inch square on lightly floured surface; wrap in plastic wrap and refrigerate 1 hour. (At this point, dough can be refrigerated 2 to 3 days, or frozen. If frozen, thaw in refrigerator; remove from refrigerator 30 minutes before rolling.) Roll dough to 9-inch square on lightly floured surface. Cut into 4 equal-size squares, then cut each square into 8 strips. Place strips on ungreased baking sheet; bake in preheated 400°F oven 10 to 12 minutes or until light brown.

Makes 32 appetizers

Note: Cheese straws can be made 2 days in advance of serving, then stored in airtight container. Or wrap tightly and freeze. To reheat baked cheese straws, place on ungreased baking sheet; bake in preheated 300°F oven 5 minutes.

Nutty Chicken Wings

18 broiler-fryer chicken wings, disjointed, tips discarded
2 eggs
1 tablespoon vegetable oil
1 teaspoon salt
1/4 teaspoon pepper
1 cup fine, dry bread crumbs
1 cup finely chopped walnuts
Honey Mustard Dip (recipe follows)

In shallow bowl, beat together eggs, oil, salt and pepper. In second shallow container, place bread crumbs and nuts; mix well. Dip wing pieces in egg mixture, then in crumb mixture, 2 or 3 at a time, turning to coat on all sides. Place wings in greased shallow baking pan. Bake in 400°F oven 30 minutes or until brown and fork tender.

Makes 36 appetizers

Honey Mustard Dip

In small bowl, mix together 1 cup mayonnaise, 2 tablespoons honey, 1 tablespoon prepared mustard, 1/2 teaspoon coriander and 1/8 teaspoon ground red pepper.

Favorite recipe from **Delmarva Poultry Industry**

Vegetable Pita Pizza

1 can (15 ounces) tomato sauce
3/4 teaspoon DURKEE© Gourmet Basil Leaves, divided
1/4 teaspoon DURKEE© Gourmet Garlic Powder
3 (6-inch) pita bread rounds
1 cup (4 ounces) shredded mozzarella cheese
2 1/2 cups assorted cut-up vegetables (zucchini, mushrooms, red or yellow bell pepper, broccoli or carrots)
6 tablespoons (1 1/2 ounces) grated Parmesan cheese

In small saucepan, combine tomato sauce, 1/4 *teaspoon* basil and garlic powder. Simmer 5 minutes, stirring occasionally. With knife, separate each pita bread into two rounds. Place on baking sheet, unbrowned side up; toast in 400°F oven for 5 minutes or until edges are golden brown. Spoon about 1/4 cup tomato sauce on each pita round. Divide mozzarella cheese and vegetables evenly between pitas; sprinkle each with a pinch of remaining 1/2 *teaspoon* basil and 1 tablespoon Parmesan cheese. Bake, uncovered, at 400°F for 10 minutes or until cheese is golden. Cut each pita into 4 wedges.

Makes 24 servings

Spicy Beef Saté

1 cup chopped scallions
1/2 cup A.1.® Steak Sauce
1/2 cup chunky or creamy peanut butter
1/4 cup lemon juice
1/4 cup firmly packed brown sugar
1/4 cup vegetable oil
1/4 teaspoon crushed red pepper
2 cloves garlic, crushed
2 pounds flank steak, cut crosswise into strips

In large glass baking dish, combine scallions, steak sauce, peanut butter, lemon juice, brown sugar, oil, red pepper and garlic until well blended. Add steak; cover and marinate at least 2 hours or overnight, stirring occasionally.

Thread steak strips onto 4-inch-long skewers. Grill or broil meat 4 inches from heat source for 10 to 20 minutes or until done, turning and brushing with marinade often. Arrange on serving platter.

Makes 4 dozen appetizers

Reuben Rolls

Reuben Rolls

- ⅓ cup HELLMANN'S® or BEST FOODS® Real, Light or Cholesterol Free Reduced Calorie Mayonnaise
- 1 tablespoon Dijon-style mustard
- ½ teaspoon caraway seeds
- 1 cup (4 ounces) cooked corned beef, finely chopped
- 1 cup (4 ounces) shredded Swiss cheese
- 1 cup sauerkraut, rinsed, drained and patted dry with paper towels
- 1 package (10 ounces) refrigerated pizza crust dough

In medium bowl combine mayonnaise, mustard and caraway seeds. Add corned beef, cheese and sauerkraut; toss to blend well. Unroll dough onto large ungreased cookie sheet. Gently stretch to 14×12-inch rectangle. Cut dough lengthwise in half. Spoon half of the filling onto each piece, spreading to within 1 inch of edges. From long side, roll each jelly-roll style; pinch to seal edges. Arrange rolls, seam-side down, 3 inches apart. Bake in 425°F oven 10 minutes or until golden brown. Let stand 5 minutes. Cut into 1-inch slices.

Makes about 30 appetizers

Hawaiian Pineapple Pizza

Preparation Time: 15 minutes
Cooking Time: 10 minutes

- 1 long loaf (1 pound) French bread
- 1½ cups pizza sauce
- 4 ounces Canadian bacon, slivered
- 1 small DOLE® Green Bell Pepper, sliced
- 1 can (20 ounces) DOLE® Pineapple Tidbits, drained
- 2 cups shredded mozzarella cheese

- Cut bread lengthwise. Spread with pizza sauce. Top with remaining ingredients.

- Broil until cheese melts.

Serves 6 to 8

Mariachi Drumsticks

1¼ cups crushed plain tortilla chips
1 package (1.25 ounces) LAWRY'S® Taco Seasoning Mix
18 to 20 chicken drummettes
Salsa

In large plastic bag, combine tortilla chips with taco seasoning mix. Dampen chicken with water and shake off excess. Place a few pieces at a time in plastic bag; shake thoroughly to coat with chips. Arrange chicken on greased microwave-safe pie plate in "spoke" pattern with thick ends of chicken toward outside edge of plate. Cover with wax paper. Microwave at MEDIUM-HIGH (70% Power) 8 to 10 minutes or until chicken is crispy, turning plate after 5 minutes. Serve with salsa for dipping.

Makes about 20 drummettes

Conventional Directions: Preheat oven to 350°. Prepare and coat chicken as above. Arrange on greased shallow baking pan; bake uncovered 30 minutes or until chicken is crispy. Serve as above.

Potato Wraps

4 small new potatoes (1½-inch diameter each)
½ teaspoon LAWRY'S® Seasoned Salt
½ teaspoon LAWRY'S® Seasoned Pepper
¼ teaspoon crushed bay leaves
8 slices bacon, cut in half crosswise

Wash potatoes and cut into quarters. Sprinkle each with a mixture of seasoned salt, seasoned pepper and bay leaves. Wrap 1 bacon piece around each potato piece. Sprinkle with any remaining seasonings. Place two sheets of paper towel in round microwave-safe pie plate. Arrange potato

pieces on plate. Microwave at HIGH (Full Power) 7 to 8 minutes or until bacon is crispy and potatoes are cooked through, turning dish after 5 minutes. Let stand on paper towels 1 minute. Serve, if desired, with sour cream and chives.

Makes 16 appetizers

Conventional Directions: Preheat oven to 400°. Prepare potatoes as above. Place in baking dish and bake uncovered 20 minutes or until bacon is crispy and potatoes are cooked through. Drain on paper towels.

Sensational Stuffed Mushrooms

Preparation Time: 20 minutes

1 pound medium mushrooms
2 tablespoons PARKAY® Margarine
1 container (8 ounces) Soft PHILADELPHIA BRAND® Cream Cheese with Chives and Onions
½ cup (2 ounces) KRAFT® 100% Grated Parmesan Cheese
2 tablespoons dry bread crumbs

• Heat oven to broil.
• Remove mushroom stems; chop enough stems to make ¼ cup.
• Saute mushroom caps in margarine 5 minutes.
• Mix soft cream cheese, Parmesan cheese and bread crumbs until well blended; stir in chopped stems.
• Fill mushroom caps.
• Broil until browned.

Makes about 2½ dozen

Top: Mariachi Drumsticks
Bottom: Potato Wraps

Appetizer Crab Balls

Appetizer Crab Balls

- ½ pound crab meat, cartilage removed
- 1½ cups soft bread crumbs
- 1 egg, slightly beaten
- 2 tablespoons HEINZ® Seafood Cocktail Sauce
- 2 tablespoons mayonnaise or salad dressing
- 2 tablespoons minced green onion
- 1 tablespoon chopped fresh parsley
- ½ teaspoon dry mustard
  Dash ground red pepper
  Dash black pepper
- 1 cup crushed potato chips
  HEINZ® Seafood Cocktail Sauce

In large bowl, combine crab meat, bread crumbs, egg, 2 tablespoons cocktail sauce, mayonnaise, green onion, parsley, mustard, red pepper and black pepper. Cover; chill at least 1 hour. Form mixture into 36 balls, using a rounded teaspoon for each. Roll in crushed chips; place on baking sheet. Bake crab balls in preheated 425°F oven, 10 to 12 minutes or until hot and golden brown. Serve with additional cocktail sauce for dipping.

Makes 36 appetizers

Chorizo Cheese Tarts

- 2 packages KEEBLER® Graham Cracker Ready-Crust® Tarts (12 tarts)
- 2 egg yolks, beaten
- 1 (12-ounce) package Mexican chorizo sausage
- ¼ cup minced onion
- 1 (16-ounce) jar or can chunky salsa
- 2 eggs, beaten
- ¾ cup (6 ounces) Mexican chihuahua or Monterey Jack cheese, grated
- ¼ teaspoon dried oregano

Heat oven to 350°. Brush tarts with a small amount of beaten egg yolks and bake 3 minutes. Remove from oven and prepare the filling.

Remove sausage from casing. Brown in skillet. Add onions and sauté until onions are soft and sausage is well done. Drain. Mix salsa with remaining eggs. Spoon sausage and onion mixture into tart shells. Pour salsa-egg mixture over sausage; top with grated cheese. Sprinkle with oregano. Bake at 350° for 20 to 25 minutes or until filling is set and cheese is melted.

Makes 12 servings

Savory Sausage Swirls

- 1 pound bulk pork sausage
- ¼ cup A.1.® Steak Sauce
- ⅓ cup chopped red bell pepper
- 3 (8-ounce) cans refrigerated crescent dinner rolls

In small bowl, combine sausage, steak sauce and red pepper; set aside. Separate each can of dough into 4 rectangles; press remaining perforations to seal. Spread 2 tablespoons sausage mixture on each rectangle. Starting at short edge, roll up jelly-roll style; seal. Cut each roll into 8 pieces; place, cut-sides down, on ungreased baking sheets.

Bake at 375°F for 12 to 15 minutes or until golden brown. Serve immediately. Rolls may be wrapped in foil and frozen for up to 2 months. To serve, thaw slightly; slice and bake as above.

Makes 8 dozen appetizers

New England Maple Ribs

2 pounds spareribs, pre-cooked
³/₄ cup CARY'S®, MAPLE ORCHARDS™ or MACDONALD'S™ Pure Maple Syrup
¹/₄ cup BENNETT'S® Chili Sauce
¹/₄ cup chopped onion
1 tablespoon *each* vinegar and Worcestershire sauce
1 teaspoon dry mustard
1 clove garlic, finely chopped

Combine all ingredients except ribs; pour over ribs. Refrigerate at least 4 hours, turning occasionally. Grill or broil ribs as desired, basting frequently with sauce. Refrigerate leftovers. ***Makes 4 servings***

Asparagus Rolls

24 thin asparagus spears, trimmed to 5-inch lengths
12 slices bread
¹/₂ cup mayonnaise
2 teaspoons lemon juice
1 teaspoon DURKEE® Gourmet Tarragon Leaves
1 teaspoon DURKEE© Gourmet Dill Weed

Cook asparagus in boiling water 1 minute. Rinse with cold water. Trim crusts from bread slices. Flatten slices with rolling pin. Combine mayonnaise, lemon juice, tarragon and dill weed. Spread mixture evenly on both sides of bread. Place 2 asparagus spears on center of each bread slice. Carefully roll up and secure with wooden toothpick. Place on baking sheet. Bake at 450°F for 8 minutes or until golden. Remove toothpicks before serving. ***Makes 12 servings***

New England Maple Ribs

Fast and Easy Pizza

- 1 pound French bread loaf (approximately 18×5 inches), split horizontally and toasted
- 1½ cups (15-ounce bottle) CONTADINA® Pizza Squeeze Pizza Sauce, divided
- 2 to 3 cups pizza toppings: shredded cheeses; sliced or chopped pepperoni, ham, bell peppers, mushrooms, olives, onions, green onions; cooked crumbled Italian sausage or ground beef; pineapple chunks; CONTADINA® Italian-Style Pear-Shaped Tomatoes, drained, cut into chunks

Place French bread halves on cookie sheet or broiler pan. Spread each half with approximately *¾ cup* pizza sauce. Arrange desired toppings over sauce. Bake in preheated 350°F oven for 10 to 12 minutes or until topping is heated through. Slice each half into four servings. **Makes 8 servings**

Crispy Chicken Drummettes

Chicken Drummettes
- 2 cups CORN CHEX® brand cereal, crushed to ¾ cup
- 1 tablespoon dried parsley flakes
- ¼ teaspoon lemon pepper or black pepper
- 2 tablespoons teriyaki sauce
- 1½ pounds (about 18) chicken wing drummettes

Sauce
- ⅓ cup seedless raspberry jam or apricot jam
- ¼ cup chili sauce

To prepare Chicken Drummettes: Preheat oven to 375°. Lightly grease 13×9-inch baking pan. In shallow dish combine cereal, parsley and pepper; set aside. Place teriyaki sauce in separate shallow dish. Roll drummettes in teriyaki sauce and then cereal mixture. Place drummettes in prepared pan. Bake 40 to 45 minutes or until lightly browned.

Fast and Easy Pizza

To prepare Sauce: In small saucepan over low heat combine jam and chili sauce; heat until warm.

Makes about 18 appetizers

Microwave Directions to prepare Chicken Drummettes: Lightly grease medium microwave-safe baking dish. Follow directions above to prepare Chicken Drummettes. Microwave at 70% POWER for 18 to 20 minutes or until fully cooked.

Microwave Directions to prepare Sauce: In small microwave-safe bowl combine jam and chili sauce. Microwave on HIGH 1 to 1½ minutes or until warm.

Spinach-Cheese Boreks

Preparation Time: 30 minutes
Cooking Time: 15 minutes

 1 **container (8 ounces) PHILADELPHIA BRAND® Soft Cream Cheese with Chives & Onions**
 1 **package (10 ounces) BIRDS EYE® Chopped Spinach, thawed, well drained**
 ⅓ **cup chopped roasted red peppers, drained**
 ⅛ **teaspoon black pepper**
 9 **frozen phyllo sheets, thawed**
 6 **tablespoons PARKAY® Margarine, melted**

- Heat oven to 375°F.

- Stir cream cheese, spinach, red peppers and black pepper in medium bowl until well blended.

- Lay one sheet phyllo dough on flat surface. Brush with margarine; cut lengthwise into four 18×3⅓-inch strips.

- For each appetizer, spoon about 1 tablespoon filling about 1 inch from one end of each strip. Fold the end over filling at 45-degree angle. Continue folding as you would fold a flag to form a triangle that encloses filling.

- Repeat with remaining phyllo and filling.

Spinach-Cheese Boreks

- Place triangles on cookie sheet. Brush with margarine.

- Bake 12 to 15 minutes or until golden brown. **Makes 36**

Notes: Thaw phyllo sheets in refrigerator 8 to 12 hours before using. Because phyllo sheets dry out very quickly, have filling prepared before removing sheets from refrigerator. For best results, work quickly and keep phyllo sheets covered with damp cloth to prevent sheets from drying out.

Before making final folds of triangle, place small herb sprig on phyllo. Fold dough over herb (herb will be on top of appetizer). Bake as directed.

Deep-Fried Eggplant Sticks

3 tablespoons CHEF PAUL
  PRUDHOMME'S VEGETABLE
  MAGIC®
1 large eggplant, peeled, and
  cut into sticks measuring
  about 3 x ½ inch
1½ cups all-purpose flour
1 large egg
1 cup evaporated milk
3½ cups vegetable oil
3 cups unseasoned bread
  crumbs
  Powdered sugar

Evenly sprinkle 1 tablespoon
Vegetable Magic® over eggplant
sticks. Set aside.

Add remaining 2 tablespoons
Vegetable Magic® to flour and mix
well. Set aside.

Beat egg with evaporated milk. Set
aside.

Pour oil into 12-inch heavy skillet.
Heat over high heat until oil reaches
350°F. When oil reaches about
250°F, dredge eggplant sticks
through seasoned flour and drop
into egg-milk mixture. Then dredge
through bread crumbs, making sure
the pieces are separate and well-
coated. Fry in 350° oil a batch at a
time, 2 to 3 minutes or until golden
brown and crisp. (Make sure to turn
the pieces early in the cooking
process so they cook evenly.) Drain
on paper towels, and, while still
warm, dust with powdered sugar.
Makes 10 servings

Chicken Wings Segovia

2 pounds chicken wings
¼ cup olive or vegetable oil
8 cloves garlic, peeled
1 teaspoon flour
¼ cup chicken broth
¼ cup dry white wine
½ teaspoon TABASCO® Brand
  Pepper Sauce
3 large sprigs parsley
  Pinch saffron (optional)

Cut chicken wings at joints; discard
wing tips. In large skillet, heat oil;
add wings and garlic. Cook and stir
10 minutes, turning wings to brown
on both sides. Remove wings and
garlic; reserve. Pour off all but 2
tablespoons oil. Stir in flour; cook
1 minute. Add broth, wine and
Tabasco® Sauce. Simmer, stirring
constantly, 2 to 3 minutes, until
thickened. Return wings to skillet. In
blender or food processor, combine
cooked garlic cloves, parsley and
saffron. Process to form a paste; stir
into sauce in skillet. Simmer 5
minutes longer, until wings are
tender. Serve hot.
Makes about 20 pieces

Curried Egg Appetizers

Preparation Time: 20 minutes

6 eggs, hard-cooked
2 to 3 tablespoons cholesterol-
  free, reduced-calorie
  mayonnaise
1 tablespoon chopped chutney
1 tablespoon frozen DOLE®
  Pineapple Juice
  concentrate, thawed*
1 tablespoon minced DOLE®
  Green Onion
½ teaspoon garlic powder
¼ to ½ teaspoon curry powder

- Slice eggs in half lengthwise.
  Remove yolks, leaving whites
  intact.

- Combine egg yolks, mayonnaise,
  chutney, pineapple juice
  concentrate, onion, garlic powder
  and curry in small bowl. Mash and
  stir until smooth.

- Pipe or spoon yolk mixture into
  egg whites. Sprinkle with paprika
  or minced green onion, if desired.
  Makes 12 appetizers

*Do not reconstitute.

Seafood Pizza Primavera

- 2 (8-ounce) packages refrigerated crescent dinner rolls
- 1 (8-ounce) container BORDEN® or MEADOW GOLD® Sour Cream
- ½ cup BENNETT'S® Chili, Cocktail *or* Hot Seafood Sauce
- 4 ounces cooked small shrimp
- 4 ounces cooked or canned crab meat or imitation crab blend
- 1 cup chopped broccoli
- ½ cup sliced green onions
- ½ cup chopped green bell pepper
- ½ cup chopped red bell pepper

Preheat oven to 400°. Unroll dough; press on bottom of 15×10-inch baking sheet, pressing perforations together. Bake 10 minutes or until golden. Cool. Combine sour cream and sauce; spread over crust. Top with remaining ingredients. Chill. Cut into squares to serve. Refrigerate leftovers.

Makes one 15×10-inch pie

Mini Cheese Turnovers

- 1 package (15 ounces) refrigerated pie crusts
- ½ cup (2 ounces) shredded Cheddar cheese
- ¼ cup chopped canned green chilies, drained
- 2 tablespoons FRENCH'S® Classic Yellow® Mustard
- 2 tablespoons butter or margarine, softened

Let pie crusts stand at room temperature 20 minutes. On lightly floured board, cut out 30 circles from crusts using 2½-inch cookie cutter (reroll dough if necessary). Combine cheese, green chilies, mustard and butter; mix well. Place a scant teaspoonful on each pastry circle. Moisten edges of pastry with water. Fold over, enclosing filling; crimp edges with tines of fork. Prick top of each turnover. Place on ungreased baking sheet. Bake at 450°F for 10 to 12 minutes or until golden.

Makes about 2½ dozen turnovers (15 servings)

Seafood Pizza Primavera

Thai Wings

Thai Wings and Ribs

Preparation Time: 15 minutes
Marinating Time: 15 minutes or
overnight
Cooking Time: 30 minutes

24 **chicken wings**
 3 **pounds spareribs, cut into**
   appetizer pieces
 1 **cup frozen DOLE® Pineapple**
   Orange Juice concentrate,
   thawed*
³/₄ **cup soy sauce**
¹/₄ **cup smooth peanut butter**
¹/₄ **cup minced cilantro**
 2 **tablespoons minced ginger**
   root
 1 **clove garlic, pressed**
 2 **teaspoons sugar**
 2 **teaspoons cornstarch**

• Cut chicken wings in 3 parts;
  reserve wing tips for another use,
  such as stock. Arrange wings in
  shallow baking pan. Arrange
  spareribs in another shallow
  baking pan.

• Combine remaining ingredients,
  except cornstarch, in small bowl.
  Spoon sauce over chicken and
  ribs to cover. Cover and marinate
  in refrigerator at least 15 minutes
  or overnight.

• Drain marinade from both chicken
  and ribs into saucepan. Stir in
  cornstarch until blended. Cook,
  stirring, until sauce boils and
  thickens. Set aside.

• Bake chicken and ribs in 375°F
  oven 25 to 30 minutes. Arrange on
  platter. Serve hot or at room
  temperature.

• Spoon cooked sauce into a bowl
  and serve as dipping sauce.
  Garnish with minced cilantro, if
  desired.   ***Makes 48 appetizers***

*Do not reconstitute.

Turkey Nachos Olé

¹/₂ **pound ground turkey**
 1 **package (1.25 ounces) taco**
   seasoning mix
¹/₄ **cup water**
 1 **package (8 ounces) tortilla**
   chips
¹/₂ **cup chopped tomatoes**
¹/₄ **cup sliced green onions**
 1 **cup shredded Cheddar**
   cheese
¹/₂ **cup shredded Monterey Jack**
   cheese
   Sour Cream (optional)

Preheat oven to 400°F. In medium
skillet, brown ground turkey. Add
taco mix and water; stir well. Bring
to a boil: reduce heat and simmer
2 minutes. Drain; set aside. Arrange
tortilla chips on baking sheet or
large shallow ovenproof platter.
Layer turkey mixture, tomatoes and
green onions on top of chips. Top
with cheeses. Bake 5 to 8 minutes or
until cheese is bubbly and melted.
Serve with sour cream, if desired.
        Makes 4 to 6 servings

Individual Herb-Cheese Tortes

Preparation Time: 25 minutes

1 container (4 ounces) PHILADELPHIA BRAND® Whipped Cream Cheese with Chives
3 tablespoons KRAFT® 100% Grated Parmesan Cheese
1 tablespoon finely chopped fresh basil
1 container (4 ounces) PHILADELPHIA BRAND® Whipped Cream Cheese
2 OSCAR MAYER® Smoked Cooked Ham Slices, finely chopped
½ teaspoon coarse grind black pepper
1 box (4½ ounces) table wafer crackers
2 tablespoons finely chopped parsley
1 hard-cooked egg yolk, sieved

- Stir cream cheese with chives, parmesan cheese and basil in small bowl until well blended

- Stir plain cream cheese, ham and pepper in small bowl until well blended.

- Spread 1 teaspoon parmesan cheese mixture onto one cracker; spread 1 teaspoon ham mixture onto second cracker. Stack crackers. Repeat with remaining spreads and crackers.

- Toss together parsley and yolk in small bowl; sprinkle over appetizers. Garnish with fresh herbs, if desired. **Makes 30**

Kahlúa® Kabobs

3 pounds lean beef or lamb, cut into 1-inch strips or cubes
Green or red bell pepper chunks, onions and cherry tomatoes
¾ cup chicken broth
¾ cup chunky peanut butter
1 ounce (2 tablespoons) KAHLÚA®
1 whole dried red chile Pepper to taste
1 clove garlic
¼ teaspoon prepared horseradish

Thread meat and vegetables alternately on skewers. In blender, combine remaining ingredients; blend until smooth. Brush kabobs with sauce. Grill or broil 6 inches from heat source until meat is cooked and vegetables are fork-tender, 5 to 10 minutes for strips; 10 to 15 minutes for cubes. Serve remaining sauce for dipping.
Makes 4 to 6 servings

Individual Herb-Cheese Tortes

Nutty Blue Cheese Vegetable Dip

- 1 cup mayonnaise or salad dressing
- 1 (8-ounce) container BORDEN® or MEADOW GOLD® Sour Cream
- 1/4 cup (1 ounce) crumbled blue cheese
- 1 tablespoon finely chopped onion
- 2 teaspoons WYLER'S® or STEERO® Beef-Flavor Instant Bouillon
- 1/2 to 3/4 cup coarsely chopped walnuts
  Assorted fresh vegetables

In medium bowl, combine mayonnaise, sour cream, blue cheese, onion and bouillon; mix well. Stir in nuts; cover and chill. Stir before serving. Garnish as desired. Serve with vegetables. Refrigerate leftovers.   *Makes about 2 cups*

Tapanade Spread

- 1 can (6³/4 ounces) tuna, drained
- 1 can (2 ounces) flat anchovies, drained
- 1 cup pitted black olives
- 1/4 cup capers, drained
- 2 tablespoons olive or vegetable oil
- 2 tablespoons mayonnaise
- 1 tablespoon brandy
- 1/4 teaspoon TABASCO® Brand Pepper Sauce
  Lemon and parsley for garnish (optional)

In food processor or electric blender combine tuna, anchovies, olives and capers; process with pulsing motion 3 or 4 seconds until mixture is blended, but not smooth. Remove to mixing bowl; stir in oil, mayonnaise, brandy and Tabasco® Sauce. Spoon into serving bowl; garnish with lemon slice and parsley, if desired. Serve with crackers or crudités.
Makes about 1 cup

Spicy Dijon Dip

- 1 (8-ounce) package cream cheese, softened
- 1/4 cup GREY POUPON® Dijon or Country Dijon Mustard
- 1/4 cup dairy sour cream
- 1 tablespoon finely chopped scallions
- 1 (4¹/4-ounce) can tiny shrimp, drained *or* 1/2 cup cooked shrimp, chopped
  Sliced scallions, for garnish
  Assorted cut-up vegetables

In small bowl, with electric mixer at medium speed, blend cream cheese, mustard, sour cream and chopped scallions; stir in shrimp. Cover; chill at least 2 hours. Garnish with sliced scallions; serve as a dip with vegetables.

Makes 1¹/2 cups

Spicy Dijon Dip

Zesty Seafood Vegetable Spread

2 (8-ounce) packages cream cheese, softened

1 (8-ounce) container BORDEN® or MEADOW GOLD® Sour Cream

1 (1.7-ounce) package MRS. GRASS® Homestyle Vegetable Recipe, Soup & Dip Mix

³/₄ cup BENNETT'S® Cocktail or Hot Seafood Sauce, chilled

1 (6-ounce) can ORLEANS® or HARRIS® Fancy White Crab Meat, rinsed, drained and chilled *or* 1 (4¼-ounce) can ORLEANS® Shrimp, rinsed and soaked

In large mixer bowl, beat cheese until fluffy; beat in sour cream and dip mix. On serving plate, spread cheese mixture into 8-inch circle. Chill at least 1 hour. Just before serving, top with cocktail sauce then crab meat. Garnish as desired. Serve with assorted crackers. Refrigerate leftovers.

Makes 12 servings

Party-Stopper Spinach Dip

2 packages (10 ounces *each*) frozen chopped spinach, thawed

1 cup mayonnaise

1 cup sour cream

3 tablespoons Durkee® Gourmet Instant Minced Onion

1½ tablespoons lemon juice

1 tablespoon Durkee® Gourmet Dill Weed

1 teaspoon salt

½ teaspoon Durkee® Gourmet Parsley Flakes

¼ teaspoon Durkee® Gourmet Leaf Thyme, crumbled

Drain thawed spinach; squeeze out excess moisture and cut up finely with kitchen shears or sharp knife. Combine spinach and remaining ingredients. Cover and refrigerate 24 hours. Serve with fresh vegetables.

Makes about 3 cups

Zesty Seafood Vegetable Spread

Pineapple and Coconut Fruit Dip

1 package (8 ounces) cream
    cheese, softened
2/3 cup (5-ounce can) *undiluted*
    CARNATION® Evaporated Milk
3/4 teaspoon vanilla extract
1/2 cup sweetened coconut
1 can (8 ounces) crushed
    pineapple in heavy syrup,
    undrained
1/2 teaspoon grated orange peel
    Fresh fruit, sliced (optional)

In medium mixer bowl, beat cream cheese until fluffy. Gradually add evaporated milk and vanilla, mixing until smooth. Add coconut, pineapple with syrup and orange peel, stirring until blended. Refrigerate several hours. Serve as dip with fresh fruit, if desired.

Makes 3 cups

Additional Serving Suggestions: May also be served over fruit as a dressing, layered with fruit in parfait glasses, or served in quartered pineapple or cantaloupe halves.

Salsa Pronto

Guacamole

3 ripe medium avocados,
    seeded and peeled
2 tablespoons REALIME® Lime
    Juice from Concentrate
1/2 teaspoon garlic salt
1/2 teaspoon sugar
1/4 teaspoon pepper

With fork or blender, mash avocados. Add remaining ingredients; mix well. Chill. Serve with La Famous® Tortilla Chips, if desired. Refrigerate leftovers.

Makes about 2 cups

Variations: Add 1 or more of the following: sour cream, cooked crumbled bacon, chopped water chestnuts, chopped fresh tomato, chopped chilies.

Salsa Pronto

1 can (14½ ounces)
    DEL MONTE® Mexican Recipe
    Stewed Tomatoes
1/4 cup finely chopped onion
2 tablespoons chopped fresh
    cilantro
2 teaspoons lemon juice
1 small clove garlic, minced
1/8 teaspoon hot pepper sauce*
    Tortilla chips

Place tomatoes in blender container. Cover and process on low 2 seconds to chop tomatoes. Combine with onion, cilantro, lemon juice, garlic and pepper sauce. Add additional pepper sauce, if desired. Serve with tortilla chips.

Makes 2 cups

*Substitute minced jalapeño to taste for hot pepper sauce.

Hot Broccoli Dip

Preparation Time: 25 minutes
Cooking Time: 25 minutes
Microwave Cooking Time: 7 minutes

1 (1½-pound) round sourdough bread loaf
½ cup chopped celery
½ cup chopped red pepper
¼ cup chopped onion
2 tablespoons PARKAY® Margarine
1 pound VELVEETA® Pasteurized Process Cheese Spread, cubed
1 package (10 ounces) BIRDS EYE® Chopped Broccoli, thawed, drained
¼ teaspoon dried rosemary leaves, crushed
Few drops hot pepper sauce

- Heat oven to 350°
- Cut lengthwise slice from top of bread loaf; remove center leaving 1-inch-thick shell. Cut removed bread into bite-size pieces. Cover shell with top of bread; place on cookie sheet with bread pieces.
- Bake 15 minutes. Cool slightly.
- Saute celery, red pepper and onion in margarine. Reduce heat to low. Add process cheese spread; stir until melted.
- Stir in broccoli, rosemary and hot pepper sauce; heat thoroughly, stirring constantly.
- Spoon into bread loaf; serve hot with toasted bread pieces and vegetable dippers.

Makes 6 to 8 servings

Hot Cheddar-Bean Dip

½ cup HELLMANN'S® or BEST FOODS® Real, Light or Cholesterol Free Reduced Calorie Mayonnaise
1 can (16 ounces) pinto beans, drained and mashed
1 cup (4 ounces) shredded Cheddar cheese
1 can (4 ounces) chopped green chilies, undrained
¼ teaspoon hot pepper sauce

In medium bowl combine mayonnaise, beans, cheese, chilies and hot pepper sauce. Spoon into small ovenproof dish. Bake in 350°F oven 30 minutes or until hot and bubbly. Serve with corn or tortilla chips. ***Makes about 2½ cups***

Basil-Parmesan Dip

Preparation Time: 5 minutes

1 cup BREAKSTONE'S® Light Choice Sour Half and Half
1 cup KRAFT® Real Mayonnaise
1 cup chopped fresh basil leaves
¼ cup KRAFT® 100% Grated Parmesan Cheese
1 tablespoon chopped sun-dried tomatoes
½ teaspoon pepper

- Mix all ingredients until well blended. Refrigerate 8 hours or overnight.
- Serve with garlic toast, breadsticks or vegetable dippers.

Makes 2½ cups

Sensational Shrimp Dip

Preparation Time: 5 minutes

½ cup MIRACLE WHIP® Salad Dressing
¼ cup lemon-flavored lowfat yogurt
1 (4¼-ounce) can tiny shrimp, drained
2 tablespoons *each:* finely chopped green onion, KRAFT® Prepared Horseradish, drained
1 tablespoon catsup

- Mix together ingredients until well blended; chill. Serve with chips and vegetable dippers.

Makes 1½ cups

Layered Taco Dip

Layered Taco Dip

- **1 pound lean ground beef**
- **1 (4-ounce) can chopped green chilies, undrained**
- **2 teaspoons WYLER'S® or STEERO® Beef-Flavor Instant Bouillon**
- **1 (16-ounce) container BORDEN® or MEADOW GOLD® Sour Cream**
- **1 (1.7-ounce) package taco seasoning mix**
- **1 (16-ounce) can refried beans**
- **1 (6-ounce) container frozen avocado dip, thawed *or* 1 cup Guacamole (see page 69)**
  Shredded cheese, chopped tomatoes, sliced green onions, sliced ripe olives
  LA FAMOUS® Tortilla Chips

In large skillet, brown meat; pour off fat. Add chilies and bouillon; cook and stir until bouillon dissolves. Cool. In small bowl, combine sour cream and taco seasoning; set aside. In 7- or 8-inch springform pan or on large plate, spread beans. Top with meat mixture, sour cream mixture and avocado dip. Cover and chill several hours. Just before serving, garnish with cheese, tomatoes, onions and olives. Serve with tortilla chips. Refrigerate leftovers.
Makes 12 to 15 servings

Cheddar Beer Dip

- **1 (8-ounce) package light cream cheese, softened**
- **1/2 cup beer**
- **2 cups shredded Cheddar cheese (about 8 ounces)**
  Parsley sprig, for garnish
  Mr. PHIPP'S® Pretzel Chips, any variety

In small bowl, with electric mixer at medium speed, beat cream cheese until smooth; gradually blend in beer. Add Cheddar cheese, beating until well blended. Cover; chill 1 hour. Garnish with parsley sprig if desired. Serve as dip with pretzel chips. **Makes 2¾ cups**

French Onion Dip

2 cups sour cream
½ cup HELLMANN'S® or BEST
   FOODS® Real, Light or
   Cholesterol Free Reduced
   Calorie Mayonnaise
1 package (1.9 ounces) KNORR®
   French Onion Soup and
   Recipe Mix

In medium bowl combine sour
cream, mayonnaise and soup mix.
Cover; chill. Serve with fresh
vegetables or potato chips. Garnish
as desired.

Makes about 2½ cups

Red-Hot Dip

3 slices white bread, crusts
   trimmed
¼ cup milk
2 medium red bell peppers
¼ cup pitted green olives
1 clove garlic
2 tablespoons olive or
   vegetable oil
1 tablespoon lemon juice
½ teaspoon TABASCO® Brand
   Pepper Sauce
   Sliced olives for garnish,
   optional

Break bread into small bowl; add
milk. Soak 10 minutes. Using a long-
handled fork, hold peppers over
stove-top burner until they are
charred. Cool; peel. In food
processor or blender combine
bread mixture, peeled peppers,
green olives and garlic. Process by
pulsing (turning food processor on
and off) about 4 seconds, just until
combined. Add oil, lemon juice and
Tabasco® Sauce; process about 3
seconds longer. Spoon into serving
bowl. Cover. Let stand at least 30
minutes to blend flavors. Garnish
with sliced olives, if desired. Serve
with pita bread or fresh vegetables.

Makes about 1¼ cups

Cucumber Dill Dip

1 package (8 ounces) light
   cream cheese, softened
1 cup HELLMANN'S® or BEST
   FOODS® Real, Light or
   Cholesterol Free Reduced
   Calorie Mayonnaise
2 medium cucumbers, peeled,
   seeded and chopped
2 tablespoons sliced green
   onions
1 tablespoon lemon juice
2 teaspoons snipped fresh dill or
   ½ teaspoon dried dill weed
½ teaspoon hot pepper sauce

In medium bowl beat cream
cheese until smooth. Stir in
mayonnaise, cucumbers, green
onions, lemon juice, dill and hot
pepper sauce. Cover; chill. Serve
with fresh vegetables, crackers or
chips. Garnish as desired.

Makes about 2½ cups

Spinach Dip

1 package (10 ounces) frozen
   chopped spinach, thawed
   and drained
1½ cups sour cream
1 cup HELLMANN'S® or BEST
   FOODS® Real, Light or
   Cholesterol Free Reduced
   Calorie Mayonnaise
1 package (1.4 ounces) KNORR®
   Vegetable Soup and
   Recipe Mix
1 can (8 ounces) water
   chestnuts, drained and
   chopped (optional)
3 green onions, chopped

In medium bowl combine spinach,
sour cream, mayonnaise, soup mix,
water chestnuts and green onions.
Cover; chill. Serve with fresh
vegetables, crackers or chips.
Garnish as desired.

Makes about 3 cups

*Left to right: French Onion Dip,
Cucumber Dill Dip and Spinach Dip*

Spinach-Parmesan Dip

Preparation Time: 5 minutes plus refrigerating

1 cup MIRACLE WHIP® Salad Dressing
1 cup BREAKSTONE'S® Sour Cream
1 package (10 ounces) BIRDS EYE® Chopped Spinach, thawed, well drained
½ cup (2 ounces) KRAFT® 100% Natural Grated Parmesan Cheese
1 can (8 ounces) water chestnuts, drained, chopped
⅛ teaspoon cayenne pepper

• Mix together ingredients until well blended. Refrigerate. Serve with assorted crackers.

Makes 4 cups

Spinach-Parmesan Dip

Swiss Cheese Spread

2 cups (8 ounces) SARGENTO® Fancy Shredded Swiss Cheese
3 tablespoons sour cream
2 tablespoons minced onion
4 slices crisply cooked bacon, crumbled
½ teaspoon salt
½ teaspoon garlic powder

Combine all ingredients; beat until smooth and of a spreading consistency. Chill.

Makes about 2 cups

Mustard Dipping Sauce

2 teaspoons dry mustard
½ teaspoon salt
½ cup half-and-half or coffee cream
½ cup COCO LOPEZ® Cream of Coconut
2 egg yolks, beaten
1 tablespoon cider vinegar

In small saucepan, combine mustard and salt. Gradually add half-and-half; mix until smooth. Add cream of coconut and egg yolks; mix well. Over medium heat, cook and stir constantly until thick and bubbly. Remove from heat; stir in vinegar. Cool. Cover; refrigerate 4 hours or overnight. Serve chilled or at room temperature. Refrigerate leftovers.   ***Makes about 1 cup***

*Use only Grade A clean, uncracked eggs.

Velveeta® Salsa Dip

Velveeta® Salsa Dip

*Preparation Time: 10 minutes
Cooking Time: 10 minutes
Microwave Cooking Time: 5
minutes*

**1 pound VELVEETA® Pasteurized
Process Cheese Spread,
cubed**
1 jar (8 ounces) salsa
2 tablespoons chopped cilantro

- In saucepan, stir together process
cheese spread and salsa over low
heat until process cheese spread
is melted. Stir in cilantro.

- Serve hot with tortilla chips or
broiled green, red or yellow
pepper wedges, if desired.

Makes 3 cups

Microwave Directions: • Microwave
process cheese spread and salsa
in 1½-quart bowl on HIGH 5
minutes or until process cheese
spread is melted, stirring after 3
minutes. Stir in cilantro. • Serve as
directed.

Variations: Substitute 1 can
(14½ ounces) tomatoes, chopped,
drained, for salsa.

Substitute 1 can (10 ounces)
tomatoes and green chilies,
chopped, drained, for salsa.

Substitute Velveeta® Mexican
Pasteurized Process Cheese
Spread with Jalapeño Pepper,
cubed, for Velveeta® Pasteurized
Process Cheese Spread.

Cheddary Vegetable Dip 'n Spread

1 package (8 ounces) cream cheese, softened
1½ cups (6 ounces) shredded Cheddar cheese
2 tablespoons FRENCH'S® Bold 'n Spicy® Mustard or FRENCH'S® Classic Yellow® Mustard
1 tablespoon FRENCH'S® Worcestershire Sauce
1 tablespoon DURKEE® RedHot Cayenne Pepper Sauce
1 teaspoon garlic powder

In mixer bowl or food processor, combine cheeses; process until smooth. Add remaining ingredients; process until well blended. Serve at room temperature with crudites or spread on crackers.

Makes about 2 cups

Tangy Cheese Dip

Preparation Time: 10 minutes

10 tablespoons 1% low-fat cottage cheese
2 teaspoons red wine vinegar
¼ cup FILIPPO BERIO® Extra Virgin Olive Oil
1 teaspoon grated orange peel
1 clove garlic or shallot, minced
1 tablespoon chopped green onion
¼ teaspoon black pepper

Process all ingredients at medium speed in blender container or food processor until thoroughly blended. Use a rubber spatula to push down mixture to blend well. Serve with an assortment of fresh vegetables, whole grain crackers or pita bread wedges.   *Makes 4 servings*

Variations: Omit red wine vinegar and orange peel. Add 2 tablespoons chopped radish, 1 tablespoon chopped celery, 1 tablespoon caraway seeds and 1½ teaspoons paprika.

Omit red wine vinegar and orange peel. Add 1 tablespoon chopped fresh parsley, 1 teaspoon Dijon-style mustard, ½ teaspoon anchovy paste and ½ teaspoon dried tarragon.

Add ½ teaspoon curry powder.

Omit orange peel. Add ¼ cup chopped mushrooms and 1½ tablespoons fresh dill.

Chili con Queso

2 tablespoons CRISCO® Oil
¼ cup minced onion
1 can (7½ ounces) whole tomatoes, drained and finely chopped
1 can (4 ounces) chopped green chilies, undrained
¼ teaspoon salt
2 cups shredded Cheddar or Monterey Jack cheese (about 8 ounces)
⅓ cup whipping cream
Nacho chips

Heat Crisco® Oil in 1-quart saucepan. Add onion. Cook over medium-high heat, stirring occasionally, until onion is tender. Add tomatoes, chilies and salt.

Stir to blend and break apart tomatoes. Heat to boiling. Reduce heat to medium-low; cook, stirring occasionally, 15 minutes. Remove from heat. Stir in cheese and cream. Cook over low heat, stirring constantly, until cheese melts. Serve with nacho chips.

Makes about 1¾ cups

Hot Chili con Queso
Follow recipe above, substituting jalapeño peppers (drained) for green chilies.

Herbed Cheese Spread

Preparation Time: 20 minutes

- **1 container (8 ounces) PHILADELPHIA BRAND® "Light" Pasteurized Process Cream Cheese Product**
- **¹⁄₂ cup MIRACLE WHIP® FREE Dressing**
- **2 tablespoons *each:* chopped fresh parsley, finely chopped green onion**
- **1 tablespoon *each:* chopped fresh oregano, chopped fresh basil and chopped fresh chives**
- **1 garlic clove, minced**
- **1 teaspoon anchovy paste (optional)**
- **¹⁄₄ teaspoon pepper**

- Mix together ingredients until well blended. Pipe mixture with pastry tube fitted with star tip into Belgian endive leaves, hollowed out cherry tomatoes and hollowed out summer squash slices.

Makes 1¹⁄₄ cups

Variation: Substitute 1 teaspoon dried oregano leaves, crushed, and 1 teaspoon dried basil leaves, crushed, for 2 tablespoons fresh oregano and basil.

Creamy Chili Dip

- **2 packages (3 ounces each) cream cheese, softened**
- **1 teaspoon lemon juice**
- **¹⁄₄ cup DEL MONTE® Chili Sauce**
- **¹⁄₄ teaspoon hot pepper sauce**
- **¹⁄₄ cup diced green chiles**
- **1 tablespoon sliced green onion**

In bowl, combine cream cheese and lemon juice; beat until smooth. Add chili sauce and hot pepper sauce. Stir in green chiles and green onion. Garnish with additional green chiles and onions, if desired. Spread on crackers; serve with vegetables, seafood and chicken.

Makes ³⁄₄ cup

Herbed Cheese Spread

Mint-Nectarine Salsa

2 fresh California nectarines, chopped
1½ tablespoons chopped fresh mint
1 tablespoon lemon juice
8 fresh flour tortillas, cut into quarters or strips, warmed

In small bowl, combine all ingredients except tortillas. Cover and refrigerate. Spoon onto tortilla quarters.

Makes about 1½ cups

Serving Suggestions: Makes a delicious low-calorie topping for grilled chicken, beef, pork or fish. Also great on quesadillas.

Favorite recipe from **California Tree Fruit Agreement**

Fresh Peach Salsa

2 fresh California peaches, diced (about 1⅓ cups)
2 plums, diced (about ⅔ cup)
⅓ cup raisins
¼ cup diced red onion
1 to 2 tablespoons lemon juice
1 tablespoon chopped fresh mint
8 fresh flour tortillas, cut into quarters or strips, warmed

In medium bowl, combine all ingredients except tortillas. Cover and refrigerate. Spoon onto tortilla quarters. *Makes about 3 cups*

Tip: Best if prepared a day ahead.

Serving Suggestions: Makes a delicious low-calorie topping for grilled chicken, pork, lamb or fish. Also great on quesadillas.

Favorite recipe from **California Tree Fruit Agreement**

Pear-Pepper Salsa

2 fresh California Bartlett pears, pared, cored and diced (about 2½ cups)
⅓ cup diced red bell pepper
⅓ cup golden raisins
2 green onions, thinly sliced
1 fresh jalapeño pepper, minced *or* 1 tablespoon canned diced jalapeño
1 tablespoon white wine vinegar
2 teaspoons minced ginger root *or* ½ teaspoon ground ginger
8 fresh flour tortillas, cut into quarters or strips, warmed

In medium bowl, combine all ingredients except tortillas. Cover and refrigerate. Spoon onto tortilla quarters. *Makes about 3 cups*

Serving Suggestions: Makes a delicious low-calorie topping for grilled chicken, pork or fish. Also great on quesadillas.

Favorite recipe from **California Tree Fruit Agreement**

Neptune Crab Dip

1 package (8 ounces) cream cheese, softened
¼ cup DEL MONTE® Seafood Cocktail Sauce
¼ cup sour cream
1 tablespoon lemon juice
½ teaspoon dill weed
1 tablespoon chopped green onion
6 ounces imitation or canned crab, flaked *or* chopped cooked shrimp

In bowl, combine cream cheese, cocktail sauce, sour cream, lemon juice and dill weed; beat until smooth. Stir in onion and crab. Serve with crackers, sliced bread or vegetables. *Makes 1½ cups*

Top to bottom: Fresh Peach Salsa, Pear-Pepper Salsa and Mint-Nectarine Salsa

Clam Onion Dip

Hot Artichoke Spread

Preparation Time: 10 minutes
Cooking Time: 25 minutes

1 cup MIRACLE WHIP® Salad Dressing
1 cup (4 ounces) KRAFT® 100% Grated Parmesan Cheese
1 (14-ounce) can artichoke hearts, drained, chopped
1 (4-ounce) can chopped green chilies, drained
1 garlic clove, minced
2 tablespoons green onion slices
2 tablespoons chopped tomato

• Preheat oven to 350°.

• Mix together all ingredients except onions and tomatoes until well blended.

• Spoon into shallow ovenproof dish or 9-inch pie plate.

• Bake 20 to 25 minutes or until lightly browned. Sprinkle with onions and tomatoes. Serve with toasted bread cutouts.

Makes 2 cups

Microwave: • Mix together all ingredients except onions and tomatoes until well blended.
• Spoon into 9-inch pie plate.
• Microwave at MEDIUM (50%) 7 to 9 minutes or until mixture is warm, stirring every 4 minutes. Stir before serving. Sprinkle with onions and tomatoes. Serve with toasted bread cutouts.

Clam Onion Dip

1 (16-ounce) container BORDEN® or MEADOW GOLD® Sour Cream
1 or 2 (6½-ounce) cans SNOW'S® or DOXSEE® Minced Clams, drained
1 (1.5-ounce) package MRS. GRASS® Onion Dip 'n Soup 'n Recipe Mix
3 tablespoons REALEMON® Lemon Juice from Concentrate
2 to 3 teaspoons prepared horseradish

In medium bowl, combine ingredients; mix well. Chill. Stir before serving. Serve with assorted fresh vegetables. Refrigerate leftovers. ***Makes about 2½ cups***

Moroccan Tomato Dip

- 1 cup (8-ounce can) CONTADINA® Tomato Sauce
- ¾ cup low-sodium garbanzo beans, rinsed and drained
- ½ cup (4 ounces) nonfat plain yogurt
- 2 tablespoons minced green onion
- 1 tablespoon finely chopped parsley
- 1½ teaspoons garlic powder
- 1 teaspoon prepared horseradish
- 1 teaspoon ground cumin
- 1 teaspoon curry powder
- ½ teaspoon paprika
  Pita Chips (recipe follows)

In blender container, process tomato sauce, garbanzo beans, and yogurt until smooth and creamy. Pour into small bowl. Stir in onion, parsley, garlic powder, horseradish, cumin, curry powder, and paprika. Cover and refrigerate 8 to 24 hours to allow flavors to blend. Serve with Pita Chips or crisp vegetable dippers.

Makes 2 cups

Pita Chips
Cut pita bread into wedges; separate each wedge into 2 pieces. Place on cookie sheet and brush with fresh lemon juice. Sprinkle with salt-free herb mixture of your choice. Bake in preheated 375°F oven for 7 to 9 minutes or until crisp.

Moroccan Tomato Dip

Zesty Snack Mix

  8 cups prepared popcorn
1½ cups dry roasted unsalted
     mixed nuts
  3 tablespoons BLUE BONNET®
     Margarine, melted
  2 tablespoons GREY POUPON®
     Dijon Mustard
  1 (0.7-ounce) package Italian
     salad dressing mix
  1 cup seedless raisins

In large bowl, combine popcorn
and nuts; set aside.

In small bowl combine margarine,
mustard and salad dressing mix.
Pour over popcorn mixture, tossing to
coat well. Spread in 15½×10½×1-
inch baking pan. Bake at 325°F for
15 minutes, stirring after 10 minutes.
Remove from oven; stir in raisins.
Spread on paper towels to cool.
Store in airtight container.

Makes about 6 cups

Kahlúa® Caramel Popcorn

  2 quarts popped popcorn
  1 cup granulated sugar
½ cup KAHLÚA®
  2 tablespoons cider vinegar
  3 tablespoons butter or
     margarine
¾ cup cashews *or* ⅓ cup
     chopped candied cherries

In shallow pan, keep popped
popcorn warm in 175°F oven. Bring
sugar, Kahlúa® and vinegar to a
boil, stirring until sugar dissolves.
Add butter. Insert candy
thermometer; bring to hard crack
stage (300°F). Pour over warm
popcorn; stir to coat evenly. Add
nuts or cherries. Cool. Store in
airtight container.

Makes about 2 quarts

Candied Walnuts

  2 cups sugar
½ cup water
  1 teaspoon vanilla
  4 cups walnut halves and pieces

Bring sugar and water to a rolling
boil. Boil 1 minute. Stir in vanilla and
walnuts; stir until coating sets.
Spread on cookie sheet to cool.

Makes 1 pound

Orange Candied Walnuts: Use ½ cup
orange juice in place of water and
1 teaspoon orange extract in place
of vanilla. Cook as directed.

Spiced Walnuts: Add 1 teaspoon
each ground cinnamon and
nutmeg to sugar mixture. Cook as
directed.

Sour Cream Walnuts: Substitute ½
cup sour cream or plain yogurt for
water. Cook as directed.

Favorite recipe from **Walnut Marketing
Board**

Zesty Snack Mix

Left: Holiday Trail Mix; Right: Festive Stuffed Dates

Holiday Trail Mix

Preparation Time: 5 minutes

**1 box (8 ounces) DOLE®
  Chopped Dates
1 cup DOLE® Whole Almonds,
  toasted
1 cup DOLE® Raisins
1 cup dried banana chips
1 cup dried apricots
¹/₂ cup sunflower seed nuts**

• Combine all ingredients. Store in
  closed container in refrigerator.
  Will keep for 2 weeks.
    Makes 11 (¹/₂-cup) servings

Festive Stuffed Dates

Preparation Time: 25 minutes

**1 box (8 ounces) DOLE® Whole
  Pitted Dates
1 package (3 ounces) light
  cream cheese
¹/₄ cup powdered sugar
  Zest from 1 DOLE® Orange**

• Make slit in center of each date.

• Combine cream cheese,
  powdered sugar and 1
  tablespoon orange zest. Fill center
  of each date with cream cheese
  mixture. Refrigerate.

• Dust with additional powdered
  sugar just before serving if desired.
    Makes about 27 stuffed dates

Cheese Popcorn

**2 quarts popped popcorn
¹/₃ cup butter or margarine
¹/₂ cup SARGENTO® Parmesan,
  Parmesan and Romano or
  Italian-Style Grated Cheese**

Spread freshly popped popcorn in
flat pan; keep hot and crisp in
200°F oven. Melt butter; add grated
cheese. Pour mixture over popcorn.
Stir until evenly coated with cheese
mixture.   ***Makes 2 quarts***

Spiced Mixed Nuts

3 tablespoons butter or
    margarine
1 envelope LIPTON® Golden
    Onion Recipe Soup Mix
¼ cup sugar
1 teaspoon ground cumin
    (optional)
1 jar (8 ounces) unsalted dry
    roasted mixed nuts

In large skillet, melt butter and stir in golden onion recipe soup mix thoroughly blended with sugar and cumin. Add nuts and cook over medium heat, stirring constantly, 5 minutes or until nuts are thoroughly coated with soup mixture and golden brown. Serve warm or spread nuts on baking sheet to cool. Store in airtight container up to 2 weeks. **Makes 2½ cups**

Crispy Bagel Chips

1 envelope LIPTON® Golden
    Onion Recipe Soup Mix
½ cup butter or margarine,
    melted
1 teaspoon basil leaves
½ teaspoon oregano leaves
¼ teaspoon garlic powder
4 to 5 plain bagels, cut into
    ⅛-inch slices

Preheat oven to 250°F. In small bowl, thoroughly blend all ingredients except bagels; generously brush on both sides of bagel slices. On two ungreased baking sheets, arrange bagel slices and bake 50 minutes or until crisp and golden. Store in airtight container up to 1 week.
Makes about 28 chips

Mexican Chili Walnuts

2 egg whites, slightly beaten*
1½ teaspoons ground cayenne
    pepper
1 tablespoon chili powder
2 teaspoons ground cumin
2 teaspoons salt
4 cups (1 pound) walnut halves
    and pieces

Coat large, shallow baking pan with non-stick vegetable spray. Mix egg whites with spices. Stir in walnuts and coat thoroughly. Spread in prepared pan. Bake in 350°F oven 15 to 18 minutes or until dry and crisp. Cool completely before serving. Store in airtight container.
Makes 4 cups

Microwave Directions: Combine as above. On microwave-safe plate microwave on HIGH in 4 or 5 batches for 2 to 3 minutes each, until dry and crisp. Cool completely.

*Use only clean, uncracked eggs.

Note: Best if made at least one day ahead. Flavors intensify overnight.

Favorite recipe from **Walnut Marketing Board**

Top: Spiced Mixed Nuts
Bottom: Crispy Bagel Chips

Peppered Pecans

- 3 tablespoons butter or margarine
- 3 cloves garlic, minced
- 1½ teaspoons TABASCO® Pepper Sauce
- ½ teaspoon salt
- 3 cups pecan halves

Preheat oven to 250°F. In small skillet melt butter. Add garlic, Tabasco® Sauce and salt; cook 1 minute. Toss pecans with butter mixture; spread in single layer on baking sheet. Bake 1 hour or until pecans are crisp, stirring occasionally.

Makes 3 cups

Easy Caramel Popcorn

Preparation Time: 20 minutes
Baking Time: 60 minutes, plus cooling

- 3 quarts popped popcorn
- 3 cups unsalted mixed nuts
- 1 cup packed brown sugar
- ½ cup KARO® Light or Dark Corn Syrup
- ½ cup MAZOLA® Margarine
- ½ teaspoon salt
- ½ teaspoon baking soda
- ½ teaspoon vanilla

Preheat oven to 250°F. In large roasting pan combine popped popcorn and nuts. Place in oven while preparing glaze. In medium saucepan combine brown sugar, corn syrup, margarine and salt. Stirring constantly, bring to boil over medium heat. Without stirring, boil 4 minutes. Remove from heat; stir in baking soda and vanilla. Pour over warm popcorn and nuts; toss to coat well. Bake 60 minutes, stirring every 15 minutes. Cool; break apart. Store in tightly covered container.

Makes 4 quarts

Mexicali Crunch

Preparation Time: 20 minutes
Baking Time: 60 minutes, plus cooling

- 4 cups corn flakes
- 2 quarts popped popcorn
- 3 cups corn or tortilla chips
- 1 cup roasted peanuts
- ½ cup MAZOLA® Margarine
- ½ cup KARO® Light or Dark Corn Syrup
- ¼ cup packed brown sugar
- 1 package (1.25 ounces) taco seasoning mix

Preheat oven to 250°F. In large roasting pan combine corn flakes, popped popcorn, corn chips and peanuts. In medium saucepan combine margarine, corn syrup, brown sugar and taco seasoning. Bring to boil over medium heat, stirring constantly. Pour over corn flake mixture; toss to coat well. Bake 60 minutes, stirring every 15 minutes. Cool, stirring frequently. Store in tightly covered container.

Makes about 4 quarts

Microwave Directions: In large roasting pan combine corn flakes, popped popcorn, corn chips and peanuts. In 1-quart microwavable bowl combine margarine, corn syrup, brown sugar and taco seasoning. Microwave on HIGH (100%) 2 to 4 minutes or until mixture boils, stirring once. Pour over corn flake mixture; toss to coat well. Bake as above.

Note: For a Texicali version of this spicy snack, substitute 5 tablespoons of chili seasoning mix for the taco seasoning.

Top: Mexicali Crunch
Bottom: Easy Caramel Popcorn

Seasoned Parmesan Popcorn

Seasoned Parmesan Popcorn

Preparation Time: 5 minutes

¹⁄₄ cup PARKAY® Margarine,
  melted
1¹⁄₂ teaspoons Mexican seasoning
2 quarts popped popcorn
¹⁄₂ cup (2 ounces) KRAFT® 100%
  Grated Parmesan Cheese

• Combine margarine with Mexican
  seasoning; mix well. Drizzle over
  popcorn; mix well.
• Add cheese; toss to coat evenly.

Makes 2 quarts

Variation: Substitute 1 teaspoon
coarse ground pepper and
¹⁄₂ teaspoon garlic powder for
Mexican seasoning.

Apricot Raisin Popcorn

6 cups popped popcorn
³⁄₄ cup unsalted dry roasted
  peanuts
¹⁄₂ cup DEL MONTE® Seedless
  Raisins
¹⁄₂ cup DEL MONTE® Dried
  Apricots, cut in quarters
2 tablespoons butter or
  margarine, melted
¹⁄₂ teaspoon vanilla extract

Combine popcorn, peanuts and
fruit. Blend butter and vanilla; drizzle
over popcorn mixture. Toss well.

Makes 7 cups

Fiery Garlic Bagel Thins

5 bagels
1/2 cup butter or margarine
6 cloves garlic, minced
2 tablespoons lemon juice
1/2 teaspoon TABASCO® Brand
   Pepper Sauce
Salt to taste

Preheat broiler. Slice bagels crosswise into fifths. In small saucepan, melt butter with garlic and simmer over very low heat for 2 minutes or until garlic has softened. Add lemon juice, Tabasco® Sauce and salt to taste. Liberally brush one side of each bagel with lemon-garlic butter. Broil bagels on one side until golden. Watch carefully; this takes only a minute. Turn bagels over and broil until golden. Serve hot or store in airtight container.

Makes 25 bagel thins

Sweet Potato Chips

1 large sweet potato
   CRISCO® Shortening for deep
   frying
   Salt (plain, onion, garlic or
   seasoned)

1. Pare potato with vegetable peeler, then pull vegetable peeler down length of potato making long, thin strips.

2. Heat a 1 1/2-inch layer of Crisco® to 365°F in deep heavy saucepan.

3. Add about 1 cup of potato strips to hot Crisco®. Fry for 1 minute or until light golden brown.

4. Remove strips from Crisco® with slotted spoon and drain on paper towels.

5. Sprinkle with desired salt before serving. **Makes 4 servings**

Toasted Sesame Seed Wafers

1/4 cup sesame seeds
1 1/2 cups all-purpose flour
3/4 teaspoon salt
1/8 teaspoon paprika
   Dash garlic powder
1/2 cup BUTTER FLAVOR CRISCO®
3 to 4 drops red pepper sauce
4 tablespoons cold water
1 tablespoon milk

Preheat oven to 375°F. Spread sesame seeds in 8-inch square baking pan. Bake for 6 to 10 minutes or until golden brown. Transfer to small dish; set aside.

In medium mixing bowl combine flour, salt, paprika and garlic powder. Cut in Butter Flavor Crisco® using pastry blender or 2 knives to form coarse crumbs. Stir in 3 tablespoons toasted sesame seed. Add red pepper sauce to 4 tablespoons water. Add liquid, 1 tablespoon at a time, mixing with fork until particles are moistened and cling together. Form dough into ball.

Roll dough 1/8 inch thick on lightly floured board. Cut with 2- or 2 1/2-inch cookie cutter. Transfer cutouts to ungreased baking sheet. Brush with milk. Sprinkle lightly with remaining sesame seeds. Bake at 375°F for 12 to 15 minutes or until light golden brown. Cool. Store in covered container.

Makes 4 to 4 1/2 dozen wafers

Spicy Turkey and Spinach Triangles

- 1 pound GROUND TURKEY
- ½ cup onion, finely chopped
- ⅓ cup red bell pepper, finely chopped
- 2 cloves garlic, minced
- ¼ teaspoon pepper
- ¼ pound medium-size mushrooms, quartered
- 1 package (10½ ounces) frozen spinach, defrosted and well drained
- 1 cup reduced-fat mozzarella cheese, shredded
- 3 packages (9½ ounces each) refrigerated pastry pockets

1. Preheat oven to 375°F.

2. In large non-stick skillet, over medium-high heat, cook and stir turkey, onion, bell pepper, garlic and pepper until turkey is no longer pink. Add mushrooms and cook 1 minute. Fold in spinach; cook 1 to 2 minutes or until most of the liquid is absorbed. Stir in cheese; remove from heat and set aside.

3. Unroll pastry, separating each package into 4 squares. Place on greased 15×10-inch jelly-roll pan. Stretch pastry slightly to shape squares.

4. Place ⅓ cup filling on one corner of each square. Fold opposite corner of dough over filling to form a triangle; press edges with fork to seal. Cut 3 (½-inch) slits in top of each triangle to allow steam to escape. Bake 12 to 15 minutes or until golden brown. Remove triangles from pan and cool on wire rack.

5. Serve triangles with Dijon-style mustard, if desired.

Makes 12 servings

Favorite recipe from **National Turkey Federation**

Taco Snack Mix

- 4 cups SPOON SIZE® Shredded Wheat
- 4 cups pretzel sticks
- 4 cups tortilla chips
- 1 (1¼-ounce) package ORTEGA® Regular or Hot & Spicy Taco Seasoning Mix
- ¼ cup BLUE BONNET® Margarine, melted

In large bowl, combine cereal, pretzels, tortilla chips and taco seasoning mix. Drizzle with margarine, tossing to coat well. Store in airtight container.

Makes 12 cups

Cheesy Potato Skins

Preparation Time: 20 minutes

- 4 large baking potatoes, baked Oil
- ¼ pound VELVEETA® Pasteurized Process Cheese Spread, cubed
- 2 tablespoons chopped red or green pepper
- 2 OSCAR MAYER® Bacon Slices, crisply cooked, crumbled
- 1 tablespoon green onion slices Sour Cream

- Heat electric broiler (not necessary to heat gas broiler).

- Cut potatoes in half lengthwise; scoop out centers, leaving ¼-inch shell. Cut shells in half crosswise.

- Fry in deep hot oil, 375°, 2 to 3 minutes or until golden brown; drain. Place on cookie sheet.

- Top with process cheese spread; broil until process cheese spread begins to melt.

- Top with remaining ingredients.

Makes 16 appetizers

Taco Snack Mix

Acknowledgments

The publishers would like to thank the companies and organizations listed below for the use of their recipes in this publication.

Best Foods, a Division of CPC International Inc.
Borden Kitchens, Borden, Inc.
California Tree Fruit Agreement
Carnation, Nestlé Food Company
Checkerboard Kitchens, Ralston Purina Company
Chef Paul Prudhomme's Magic Seasoning Blends™
Contadina Foods, Inc., Nestlé Food Company
Delmarva Poultry Industry, Inc.
Del Monte Foods
Dole Food Company, Inc.
Filippo Berio Olive Oil
Florida Department of Citrus
The Fresh Garlic Association
Heinz U.S.A.
Kahlúa Liqueur

Keebler Company
Kraft General Foods, Inc.
Lawry's® Foods, Inc.
Thomas J. Lipton Co.
M&M/Mars
McIlhenny Company
Nabisco Foods Group
National Broiler Council
National Live Stock & Meat Board
National Pork Producers Council
National Turkey Federation
North Dakota Wheat Commission
The Procter & Gamble Company, Inc.
Reckitt & Colman, Inc.
Sargento Cheese Company, Inc.
USA Rice Council
Walnut Marketing Board
Wisconsin Milk Marketing Board

Photo Credits

The publishers would like to thank the companies and organizations listed below for the use of their photographs in this publication.

Best Foods, a Division of CPC International Inc.
Borden Kitchens, Borden, Inc.
California Tree Fruit Agreement
Chef Paul Prudhomme's Magic Seasoning Blends™
Contadina Foods, Inc., Nestlé Food Company
Del Monte Foods
Dole Food Company, Inc.
Heinz U.S.A.

Kraft General Foods, Inc.
Lawry's® Foods, Inc.
Thomas J. Lipton Co.
M&M/Mars
Nabisco Foods Group
National Live Stock & Meat Board
The Procter & Gamble Company, Inc.
Reckitt & Colman, Inc.
USA Rice Council
Walnut Marketing Board